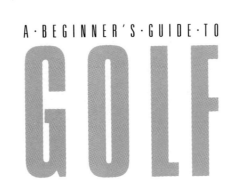

A·BEGINNER'S·GUIDE·TO

GOLF

A · BEGINNER'S · GUIDE · TO

GOLF

NICK LUMB

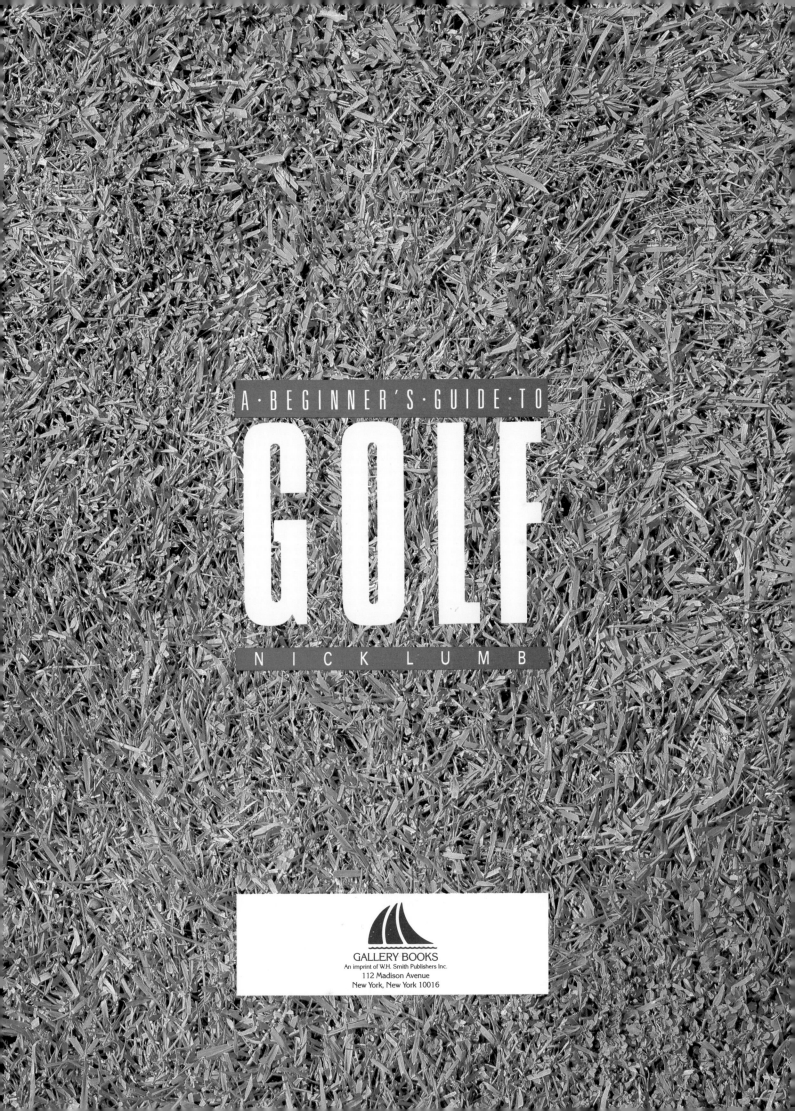

GALLERY BOOKS
An imprint of W.H. Smith Publishers Inc.
112 Madison Avenue
New York, New York 10016

A QUINTET BOOK
produced for
GALLERY BOOKS
An imprint of W. H. Smith Publishers Inc.
112 Madison Avenue
New York, New York 10016

ISBN 0–8317–4955–5

This book was designed and produced by
QUINTET PUBLISHING LIMITED
6 Blundell Street
London N7

DESIGNER Linda Moore
ART DIRECTOR Peter Bridgewater
EDITORS Peter Arnold, Shaun Barrington
PHOTOGRAPHER Ian Howes
ILLUSTRATOR Rob Schone

Typeset in Great Britain by
Central Southern Typesetters, Eastbourne
Manufactured in Hong Kong by
Regent Publishing Services Limited
Printed in Hong Kong by
Leefung-Asco Printers Limited

The author would like to thank John King for
his invaluable assistance in the preparation of
this book.

● CONTENTS ●

INTRODUCTION

Golf is one of the world's fastest growing sports. Television, with its knowledgeable commentators and probing cameras, has brought international championships into the home. The tournament players themselves are marvellous ambassadors for the sport; they behave impeccably and bring excitement to every event. By its very nature, golf is a game which breeds good manners and courtesy.

This is one sport which the whole family can play together. It is a game that you can play on your own, or as a member of a group. Beginners everywhere are queuing up to learn the skills needed to take up the challenge of the golf course. The working week is getting shorter: which means more players. The retirement age is getting lower: which means more players. People are now more than ever aware of the need for exercise: which means more players. Everywhere, people are taking up this fabulous game.

The system of handicapping in golf enables players of varying abilities to compete on level terms: one of golf's particular advantages. Another asset is the great variety of courses across the world, each posing different problems to the golfer; but even if you were to stick to your local course for a lifetime, no two rounds would be identical. The shot permutations needed to master 18 holes are never quite the same twice; and the variety of skills, the ingenuity and judgement employed each time you take up the challenge, can be endlessly honed and improved.

LEFT One of golf's particular attractions is the beauty and tranquility of the courses themselves; but those seemingly innocuous greens and fairways pose a tremendous challenge to your physical coordination, your skill and nerve.

ABOVE It is possible to buy just one secondhand club with which to begin learning the game – a 5-iron is fine – along with a putter. By hiring or borrowing clubs at the outset, you will not find yourself stuck with expensive equipment ill-suited to your game at a later date.

THE EQUIPMENT

When you are choosing equipment to play golf, the points to bear in mind are the same as for any other pastime: do not buy more than you need to start off with, make sure that what you do buy will have enough use to justify the initial outlay, and above all, ensure that the equipment suits your physique and style of play.

RIGHT A set of irons consists of nine clubs. A half set is either the four even, or the five odd numbers. A wood and a putter make up the half-set.

Golf, and the equipment used to play it, have changed out of all recognition since the birth of the game. The days of playing with little more than wooden sticks have given way to current demands for equipment built to complex technical specifications. The development of equipment has matched the changes in the game and in the courses.

In the early days, when golfers used clubs with hickory shafts, their swings had to suit the characteristics of the shaft. The hickory shaft had torque, or twist, giving a natural turning in the shaft. Yesterday's golfer did not work against this, but turned it to his advantage. His swing plane was flatter, with a lot more hand and arm action. Opening up the club-face on the way back, he then brought it square to the ball and closed it on the way through. This meant the player had to aim to the right to allow for the draw that this swing had fashioned. This gave the shot over-spin, or top-spin, and so the run factor was very important. Neither fairways nor greens were watered, so golf courses suited the type of game where the object was to make the ball run after pitching. The ball used to run and run on the courses of the day.

With the introduction of steel shafts without torque, the golf swing had to change to suit the clubs and the modern square-to-square method came into favour. It eliminated the opening and closing of the club-face

This coincided with the change in golf course practice. Watered greens came first, soon to be followed by watered fairways. Golf balls do not run as far on lush grass, so the swing concept changed, to provide height and flight.

When choosing equipment, you may start to play golf with a single club, a half-set or a full set, with new or used clubs. Many beginners buy a single used iron to begin swinging into the game to see if they enjoy it.

If you begin with just one new club, buy it from a source – a professional or sports shop – which can supply matching clubs singly. You can build up your set as your needs gradually grow.

If you decide on a half-set, bear in mind that you may not be able to add matching clubs at a later date. Often manufacturers change models.

The third option is to buy a full set, new or used, straight away. A full set contains a maximum of 14 clubs. It usually consists of nine irons, four woods and a putter. Make sure, when choosing a full set, that the irons all match. Mixed irons do not constitute a set.

● THE PUTTER ●

Many golfers think that a putter has no loft, but it actually has between two and four degrees. When struck with a putter, the ball skids for the first 20 per cent of its journey and then rolls, with over-spin, the remaining 80 per cent.

Putters come in many shapes and sizes. Whatever the design of the putter you must strike the ball consistently out of the 'sweet spot'. Many putters have lines or spots to help with the lining up, and players assume that this must be the sweet spot, but this is not always correct. To find the sweet spot, most professionals hold the putter loosely between the forefinger and thumb, allowing it to hang. Then, using one of those pencils with an eraser on the end, they tap the club-face with the eraser until they find the place which feels the most solid. This place is the sweet spot.

A ball not struck with the sweet spot of the putter will lose distance. That happens to any ball struck with either the toe or heel of the putter. The longer the putt the greater the error will be.

When putting, the putter should be grounded with the sweet spot directly behind the ball.

The lengths of putter shafts vary between 33 and 36 in (84 and 91 cm). The shafts are usually stiff. The weights vary between 15 and 18 oz (425 and 510 g).

Your choice of putter should be influenced by the speed of the greens at the course where you intend to play most of your golf. If they are fast, choose a lightweight putter: the slower the surface, the heavier the putter should be.

● THE SWEET SPOT ●

To find the sweet spot of a putter, hold the putter loosely between the forefinger and thumb, allowing it to hang vertically. Using a pencil with an eraser on the end, tap the club-face with the eraser until you find the place which feels most solid. This is the sweet spot.

BELOW LEFT When you buy a full set, make sure that all the irons are by the same manufacturer and of the same model.

RIGHT The loft on the clubs decreases as their numbers decrease.

• IRONS •

There are two different ways of manufacturing iron heads for golf clubs: casting and forging.

The method for cast heads allows mass production of even complicated designs and ensures consistency of weight in each clubhead. It also means that the lofts of each set will be perfectly matched. The materials used are of hard steel, and the production methods therefore make it difficult to manufacture heads to suit players who are not of standard height and build.

Forged heads are made from softer metals. Their softness means that they can be custom-ground and shaped to suit individuals. For this reason, most touring professionals choose to play with this type of club.

• CLUBHEAD •

The long irons used for distance have the smallest numbers of the clubs in the set. The chipping, pitching and sand irons have the highest numbers. All share built-in design factors allowing the golfer to meet his individual needs. Golf clubheads come in different shapes to do different things. You must decide what you want your golf club to do. The centre of gravity and the lie of the clubhead are the important features to examine when choosing clubs to suit your physique.

The centre of gravity relates to the distribution of the weight in the clubhead. If you have trouble getting the ball into the air, you must select a club with the weight at the bottom of the clubhead. When striking the ball, the centre of gravity will be below the centre of the ball, helping to lift it in the air, and resulting in a soaring flight.

On the other hand, many golfers feel that they

The rules of golf are codified and approved by the Royal and Ancient Golf Club of St Andrews and the United States Golf Association. The rules were last overhauled (and simplified) in 1984. You should find little difficulty in learning the basics very quickly, and should carry the rule-book out on the course for reference.

If you consider for a moment the *potential* complexity of rule-making for the game of golf — what may be fair, for example, when you are faced with an impossible lie, or what happens if your ball goes out of bounds — then you will realise that the rule-book is really a surprisingly short and succinct document.

● DEFINITION OF LIE ANGLE ●

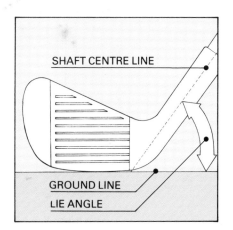

The lie angle of the clubhead is extremely important and is dependent upon the angle of swing.

hit the ball too high, and they must therefore select a club design where the weight has been positioned higher in the clubhead. When striking the ball, the centre of gravity will be above the centre of the ball. This will help to keep the ball lower in flight. If the centre of gravity lies in the middle of the blade — behind the ball — then mid-flight will be achieved.

The lie of the clubhead is the angle formed by a line through the centre of the shaft and the ground, when the clubhead is placed flat in the address position.

An upright lie is favoured by taller golfers because their hands are farther from the ground. The flatter lies put you slightly farther from the ball in the address position and are therefore more suited to the shorter golfer. If you take a club with too upright a lie for you, the heel of the clubhead will be on the ground but the toe raised off it a little. When swinging into the ball with too upright a lie, the heel will hit the ground

OPPOSITE A set of woods can consist of three or four clubs.

CLUB DESIGN AND NUMBERS (RULE 4)

All clubs you are likely to come across will of course comply with the rules; any manufacturer who is unsure about the legality of a new design must submit a proto- type to St Andrews for a rul- ing. The ruling on the *number* of clubs allowed is more important for the beginner; you can play with a maxi- mum of 14 clubs, and cannot replace a damaged club or add to your set, once you start to play, by borrowing from another player who is playing out on the course.

OPPOSITE A set of woods can consist of three or four clubs. Most modern sets have only three: the driver and the three and five woods. The driver has the biggest head and the deepest face. The clubheads become smaller as their loft increases, which gives the five wood clubhead a lower centre of gravity.

● IRONS ●

Iron NUMBER	Strong loft DEGREES	Standard loft DEGREES	Weak loft DEGREES
3	22	24	26
4	26	28	30
5	30	32	34
6	34	36	38
7	38	40	42
8	42	44	46
9	46	48	50
Pitching wedge	50	52	54
Sand wedge	54	56	58

before the ball is sent away and the 'free' toe will come round, closing the club-face and sending the ball, for a right-hander, to the left. If the lie is too flat, the opposite will happen. At the address the toe will be on the ground but the heel will be clear of it. When striking into the shot, the toe will hit the ground, spinning the heel past the toe and opening the club-face, shooting the ball to the right.

Spend some time and seek professional advice over obtaining clubs. They should suit you for length, lie, swing weight and centre of gravity. Between each number in a set of irons, there are four degrees of loft, representing 10– 12 yd (9–11 m) of flight.

The weight of each iron club increases throughout the set. In an average set, the lightest is the 3-iron at 15 oz (425 g) and each succeed- ing iron gets heavier, with the 9-iron weighing 16 oz (454 g). The sand wedge and pitching wedge are designed to be even heavier for their particu- lar roles.

● WOODS ●

There is no end to the selection of drivers and fairway clubs coming onto the golfers' market, with new designs of heads, and variations in weight displacement and shaft tensions. They are all still generally referred to as 'woods', al- though many clubs now attracting increasing support are metal-headed. These are hollow and the design places the weight around the peri- meter of the head. This helps the golfer to achieve consistency in his shots, even when he fails to strike the ball in the middle of the club- face. He also finds help from the lower centre of gravity of the clubhead, as opposed to the wooden clubhead. This sends the ball higher and makes the club easier to use. Many profes- sional golfers are switching to metal. A wider selection of lofts is now available for metal- headed clubs.

The heads of wooden clubs are still either persimmon or laminated maple. Persimmon is thought, quite wrongly, to be the harder of the two. Laminated maple has an advantage over persimmon, in that a matched set of laminated woods – a driver, a 3-wood and a 5-wood – have a greater consistency of weight. Irons should, as was emphasized, be bought in a set, but this is not a must for the woods. It is acceptable to find three unmatched clubs to do the jobs required: a driver to hit off the tee, a fairway wood to play long shots and a more lofted club for the inter- mediate shots.

A good quality set of headcovers should always be placed on these clubs to protect them from being marked by the heads of the irons when they are taken out of the bag and replaced. When the headcovers get wet, take them off after the round of golf and dry them. Leaving them wet on your clubs will cause gradual but severe deterioration in the clubhead. It can cause rust on metal heads. On persimmon, it can cause the wood to swell and with the lamin- ated clubs the polyurethane coating is attacked, ultimately causing the thinning paint to chip.

● WOODS ●

Wood NUMBER	Strong lofts DEGREES	Standard lofts DEGREES	Weak lofts DEGREES
1	10	11	12
2	12	13	14
3	15	16	17
4	18	19	20
5	21	22	23

● SHAFTS ●

A golf shaft starts as a tube about one inch (25 mm) in diameter which is drawn through a die until it is the diameter required. Shafts come in many different types, weights and flexes. The most flexible shafts are distinguished by the letter 'L' and these are put in most ladies' golf clubs. After these come the 'A' flex, suitable for the stronger lady and the slow-swinging man. The most popular flex is the 'R' flex, suitable for the majority of men. The stronger player and the player with a faster tempo to his swing will find the 'S' flex most suitable for his game, and the very strong player should use an 'X' flex. A shaft acquires its flex from the thickness of its walls. The thicker the walls, the stiffer the flex and the greater the weight. A standard men's shaft weighs between 4 and 4¼ oz (113 and 120 g).

● GRIPS ●

Grip lengths vary between 10 and 11 in (254 to 280 mm). Weights vary between 1.5 oz (43 g) for ladies and 1.65 oz (47 g) for men. Thicknesses also vary and should be chosen to suit the length of your fingers. Grip thickness is very important. If the grip is too thick, it will restrict the movement in your wrist and, if you are right-handed could cause many shots to go to the right. Similarly, a grip that is too thin will cause excessive use of the hands, forcing many bad shots to go to the left.

● CLUB SUMMARY ●

When choosing golf clubs, consider these very important points: the loft; the shape of the head; the centre of gravity (these determine the flight of the ball); the lie (to suit your posture); the weight; the flex of the shaft; the thickness of the grip (to suit your hands). If any of these aspects of the clubs is not to your liking, then you might need to have the clubs altered slightly, or, as it is known in the trade, custom-made.

Who might need custom-made clubs? The answer is every golfer, but some will benefit much more than others. People who need custom-made clubs, or clubs which can be altered, are those with longer or shorter fingers than normal, tall players with short arms and *vice versa,* those with a tendency to hook, slice, push or pull the ball.

A waterproof suit, such as the one worn here by Sandy Lyle, should not be too tight-fitting, particularly across the shoulders and under the arms.

● WATERPROOFS ●

The fun of playing golf tends to drain away when you have to play in the rain. Whether you choose to begin a round in the rain or get caught on the course when the rains arrive, you will need waterproofs as part of your golfing equipment. Some people are willing to withstand a little wetness, provided they are warm. You may prefer a suit which is windproof rather than waterproof. There is a wide choice of both waterproofs and windproofs.

When buying a suit for those windy or wet days it should not be figure-hugging. Give yourself plenty of room inside it so that your swing is not impeded and you can bend with ease. If you do not keep supple and free-moving in rainy conditions, any hopes of good golf will, literally, be a 'wash-out'. Manufacturers of wet weather clothing offer varying guarantees concerning the 'dry time' you might expect inside rainproofs. New materials developed recently are very efficient in keeping the golfer comfortable and dry. Enquire about these new light-weight suits if you plan to go 'Swinging in the Rain'. Until these new developments, waterproofs did not breathe, and perspiration trapped inside was uncomfortable. Now you can keep dry, swing your clubs with ease, and any perspiration you are generating can flow out, keeping the body temperature even.

● GLOVES ●

A glove is worn on the left hand to help the foundation of a good, firm grip at the top of the shaft. It can be of pure leather or synthetic material and the price varies accordingly. Both materials assist a non-slip left hand which is essential when you bring your right hand into the anchored left to make the grip.

Do not choose gloves which fit too sleekly. If they leave pressure marks they will be impeding circulation. Some gloves carry instructions and advice on fitting. Follow them.

ABOVE The golf umbrella is effective in heavy showers but cannot give protection in high winds. You may prefer a hat or cap which can protect your eyes against the rain and can even be an aid to concentration, particularly on the putting green, focusing attention on the ball.

RIGHT The only important choice in footwear is between spiked or non-spiked shoes.

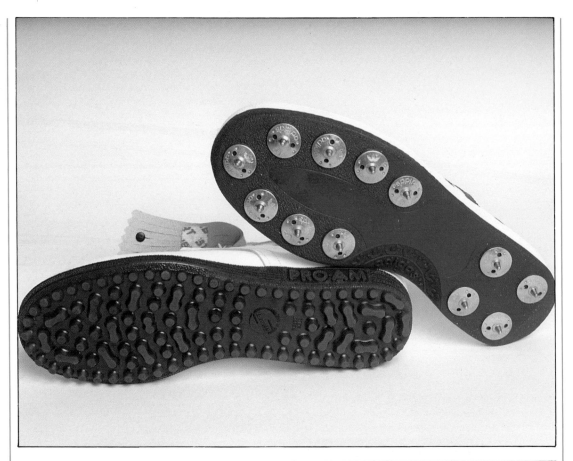

● SHOES ●

Golf professionals' shops are usually stocked with a wide choice of golf shoes in various colours. This market is highly competitive, with Far Eastern countries claiming a share. Your priority is to seek comfort. You walk a long way on a golf course (especially if you do not keep to the fairway), you climb and you descend, you stride out and you wait about. A comfortable pair of golf shoes are two good companions you should choose to take with you.

Should you buy spiked or non-spiked golf shoes? The weight of spikes makes these shoes heavier to wear. Spikes give a slightly better grip to the ground and are helpful when walking on hilly courses, but on hard fairways where they do not fully bite, they lose their advantage over the non-spiked and lighter shoe. Take care not to damage the green when wearing spikes.

The choice of shoes now available to golfers dazzles the customer. Should you buy leather or non-leather uppers, with leather or non-leather soles? Comfort is the deciding factor, plus, of course, how much you can afford to pay for it.

ABOVE Golf shoe spikes are not of course as sharp as those of an athlete's shoe. They are made of stainless steel and should not deteriorate.

• GOLF BALLS •

The game of golf has evolved around the little white ball. This book is about hitting it correctly. Take away some of the golf clubs and you still have a game. Take away the ball and you are left with practice swings. The pursuit of this ball on courses across the world has provided pleasure and despair, has led to new industries manufacturing clubs and equipment, has created thousands of jobs, has made millionaires of top players and has led to improvements in its own manufacture.

Briefly, there are three separate types of golf ball: solid, three-piece and two-piece. The solid ball is at the bottom end of the market and is favoured by many beginners, mainly because of its low price. Older golfers may remember taking golf balls to pieces, peeling off the outer covers so that they could unravel miles of rubber bands wound round the soft centre of the ball. This type of ball is still manufactured today, although its components and Balata cover have been improved by modern technology. It is known as the three-piece ball.

New technology has also given birth to the two-piece ball, which has a harder feel in its blended Surlyn cover, and is a lot less likely to be damaged by mis-hit shots. Inside the two-piece is a resilient core of blended resins.

There are two sizes of golf balls, the 1.62 and the 1.68. The numbers refer to the diameter in inches. The traditional golf ball is the 1.62 as approved by the Royal and Ancient Golf Club of St Andrews, the ruling body of golf. From America came the slightly larger 1.68. This size has now won international approval and is the only one permitted in national and international competitions. Golf ball manufacturers still produce the 1.62, but in decreasing numbers.

● THE TWO-PIECE BALL ●

This ball has a solid centre core made of moulded rubber, covered with a pigmented Surlyn cover.

● THE BALATA BALL ●

Stages of the Balata ball manufacture: the rubber centre is filled with water. Rubber bands are wound round it. The Balata outer cup has the dimples moulded in, painted, lacquered and stamped *Titleist*.

● THE SURLYN COVERED BALL ●

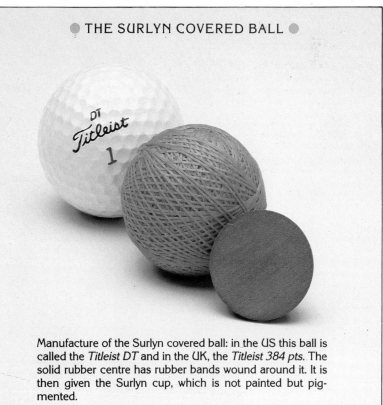

Manufacture of the Surlyn covered ball: in the US this ball is called the *Titleist DT* and in the UK, the *Titleist 384 pts*. The solid rubber centre has rubber bands wound around it. It is then given the Surlyn cup, which is not painted but pigmented.

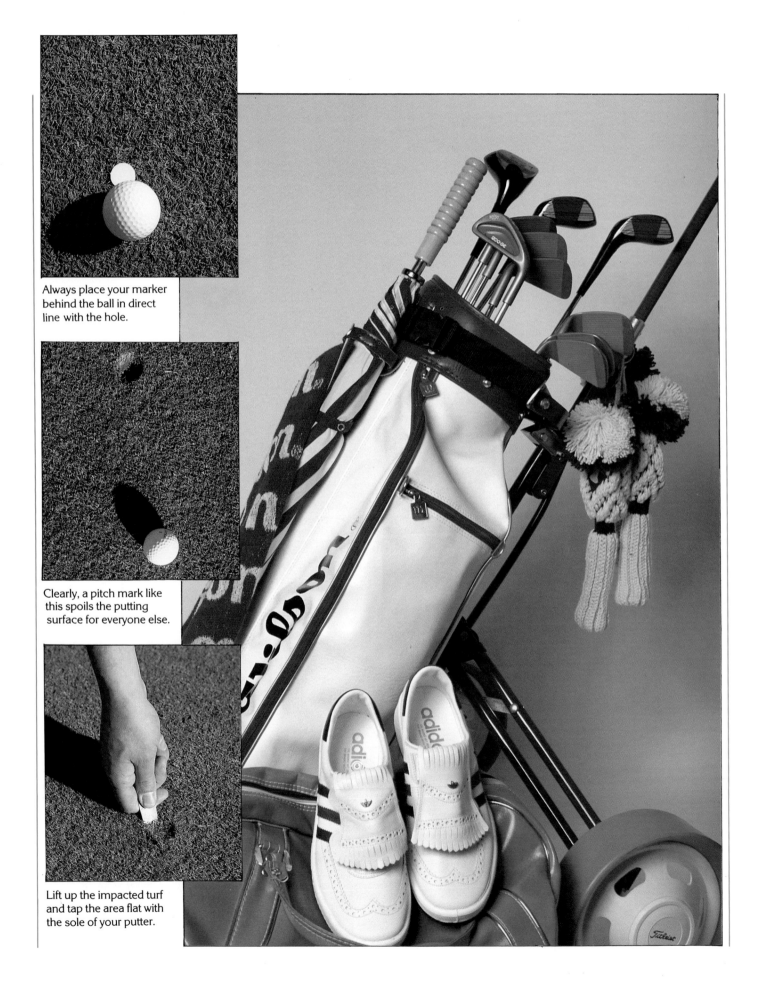

Always place your marker behind the ball in direct line with the hole.

Clearly, a pitch mark like this spoils the putting surface for everyone else.

Lift up the impacted turf and tap the area flat with the sole of your putter.

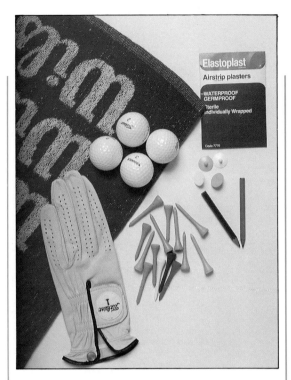

● GOLF BAGS ●

To carry or to trolley – that is the question. The best carry bags are collapsible and therefore have no supports, but a trolley bag needs some side supports to keep it firm on the trolley. When buying a carry bag lightness is the important factor. It is a long way round a golf course and, when full of the other accessories as well as the clubs, the bag is carrying quite a heavy load. A trolley bag on the other hand can be a little larger. The small amount of extra weight when placed on a trolley will not be noticed.

Many players judge a bag by how big or wide the top is. That is only half the story. The bottom is as important, if not more so. If it is too small, then the grips get jammed together and rub against each other when they are pulled out. When watching the touring professionals, weekend golfers look at the size of their golf bags and think how uncomfortable it must be for their caddies to carry them around. In fact they are well designed so that the weight is distributed evenly over the whole bag.

Whether you carry or trolley depends ultimately on your fitness and your pocket.

● TROLLEYS ●

It is a false economy to choose a trolley from the cheap range. The difference in design is usually considerable, while the difference in price is much less. Choose a trolley which you can pull standing upright.

● MISCELLANEOUS ITEMS ●

Other useful items you will require on your round include the following:

Umbrella: Be prepared for that shower which hits you on the hole furthest from the clubhouse. Remember, you may not seek shelter when playing in a competition.

Tee pegs: Both wooden and plastic pegs are available. The wooden pegs are favoured by those golfers who dislike the plastic pegs sometimes marking the faces of their woods. However they break more easily than the plastic pegs, which are cheaper and more popular.

Ball markers: Markers are small discs which are used to mark the position of the ball on the green when you have picked it up for cleaning, or because it is impeding the shots of others. They are a must for the golf bag, or better still, a handy pocket. Some ranges of golf gloves have detachable markers.

There is only one correct way to use a marker. Stand behind the ball facing the hole. Place the marker behind and underneath the ball, making sure that you do not touch the ball. Never place a marker in front of the ball, or at the side of it, because there is a risk that, with loss of concentration when studying the next putt, you could place the ball back in front of the marker. Although you may have made the error inadvertently, it could look suspiciously like an illegal trick to gain ground.

Pitchfork: A pocket pitchfork is carried by all golfers who extend courtesy to other players. A constant complaint in the locker room is aimed at golfers who have not repaired their pitch marks on the green. The ball dropping down into a soft green from its high arc makes an indentation on the putting surface. It is every golfer's duty to repair his own pitch mark.

Pencil: You must not forget a pencil for scoring.

Scorecard: Similarly, you need a scorecard bearing all the local rules, including information on those holes of the course at which shots may be claimed when playing a match.

Towel: You should carry a towel to wipe clean your golf balls and clubs.

Stretch fabric plasters: Plasters are not carried for any expected personal injuries, although sometimes sore fingers and heels may need attention. Temporary repairs to equipment can be made with this useful adhesive tape.

Book of rules: A book of rules is a must.

LEFT Important items needed when you go onto the course: a left hand glove to help give you added strength and adhesion in your grip; tee-pegs, marker, pencils, golf balls, and adhesive tape.

OPPOSITE Equipment you will need before you begin to play a round of golf. All are necessary and of equal importance to your success.

THE GOLF SHOT

If you are to establish a successful golfing technique, then you must get the basics right. This section will show you the first principles of striking the ball: how your stance, your grip and your swing are the vital elements in every shot. Get it right at this stage and you will avoid developing faults later on.

Golf is a world-wide game played by millions of people with many different standards, but they all have one thing in common – they can improve. Whatever your standard, it is hoped that this chapter will teach you through simple, easy to follow instructions, how to make your shots more consistent.

Later in the chapter, the shots themselves are analyzed, starting with the short shots on the green where all holes end, and working back

● THE TARGET LINE ●

Place two clubs on the floor parallel to each other, like railway lines, to help you to picture the target line and position your feet correctly.

The start of the address position, with the feet on one line and the club pointing square down the target line.

from flag to tee to take in the long shots. This follows the way a child is helped to gain confidence in catching a ball. The ball is not hurled at first from long distances but gently lobbed into eager but unsure hands from only a few feet. In that way, confidence is increased until the high catches are easily taken.

Unfortunately the golf shot is not as simple as catching a ball. It consists of four separate components:

Aim: This ensures that the ball will be sent in the desired direction.

Grip: This controls the clubhead.

Stance: This ensures correct positioning and posture when making the shot.

Swing: This controls the plane of attack, and ensures that the ball is hit correctly.

All four components are important and each is dependent for effectiveness upon the other three. None can be neglected if the shot is to be effective. All deserve equal thought and practice, and are dealt with separately in the following pages.

● THE AIM ●

'It's all in the mind' is a phrase used in many sports, particularly those like golf, where a stationary ball is to be hit. It leads to positive action. The idea is that you must imagine the shot to be played before addressing the ball, and you must be confident that you can make it. You picture the shot you are about to make – then go ahead and make it.

Stand directly behind the ball looking towards the flag and imagine two clubs lying on the ground going away from you like railway tracks running from the ball towards the target. One line will be the target line for the ball, the other line will be for the correct positioning of the feet. Look for this target line. If you cannot see it, a simple exercise might help. Clench the fist of the right hand, and still standing behind the ball, gently swing the arm backwards and forwards as though you were going to throw a ball underhand along a line to the target. This action helps many beginners to see the imaginary line of flight.

Stand opposite the ball at right angles to the target. Place the clubhead square behind the ball. You are now *addressing* the ball. The sole, or bottom of the club, will be sitting flat on the ground with the face square to the target, and you will be aiming correctly.

● THE CLUB-FACE ANGLE ●

The sole of the club must be flat on the floor, with the blade square to the target line.

The shorter the shot, the closer together the feet.

Swing the club to the top of the backswing; the club shaft will point towards the target, keeping the club-face square to the plane.

RIGHT When gripping the club, the back of the left hand and the palm of the right hand must point towards the target.

RIGHT The club grip lies across the left hand. The heel of the hand is on the top of the grip and the forefinger underneath, as though you were pulling a trigger.

FAR RIGHT AND INSET When the left hand is closed, the thumb and first finger should be level and the 'V' from the thumb and forefinger should point to the right shoulder.

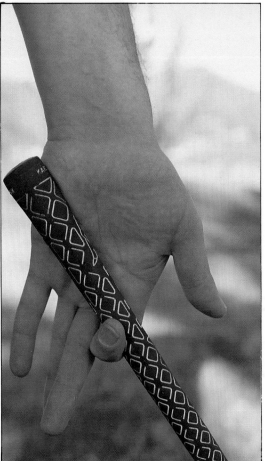

● THE GRIP ●

All the world's top golfers have one thing in common: a correct grip. Only through the correct grip can you control the clubhead. The following descriptions assume a right-handed player, and obviously should be reversed for left-handers.

Many newcomers may find adopting the correct grip uncomfortable at first, but they should persevere. It will become a natural asset.

On forming the grip, it should be firm but not white-knuckle tight. The back of the left hand and the palm of the right hand point to the target and are square with it. Both hands must work together as one unit. The swing generates the power and passes it onto the clubhead through the hands. Your clubhead fires the ball to the target.

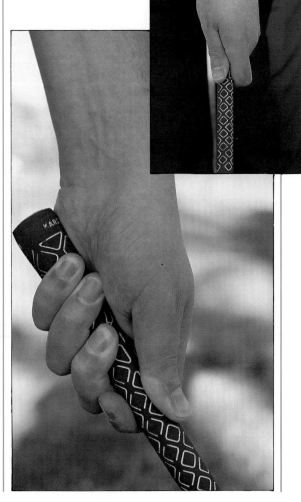

● THE LEFT HAND ●

Place your feet together at right angles to the target, with the toes pointing towards the ball, so that the ball is on a line which would pass between your feet. Drop the left arm, keeping it firm, with the back of the left hand square to the hole.

With the clubhead grounded behind the ball, place the club grip across the left hand. The butt (or the top of the club grip) will be lying snug along the palm. It is essential that the club is gripped by the fingers against the palms of the hands so that the wrist stays in a relaxed position, enabling a natural wrist-break to take place in the swing. You will see that the forefinger is underneath the grip as though about to pull a trigger. Now place the thumb on the top of the club grip and close the hand. The thumb and forefinger should be nearly level. The V created by the thumb and forefinger should be pointing between your head and right shoulder. You are now ready to bring in the right hand.

● THE RIGHT HAND ●

With the right hand, the palm points towards the target. The two middle fingers must have the control of the club. Let these two fingers grip the club and slide them up to meet the left hand, with the little finger overlapping the forefinger of the left hand. Now close the hand, with the thumb lying across the left hand side of the club grip. The V formed by the right thumb and the right forefinger should follow the same direction as the V on the left hand, i.e. it should be pointing between your head and right shoulder.

This grip is internationally known as the Vardon Grip, after its pioneer Harry Vardon, who between 1896 and 1914 won the British Open six times and in 1900 the American Open. Some beginners may discover that this grip is uncomfortable even after they have practised it for some time, so an alternative grip must be tried. Two commonly used ones follow.

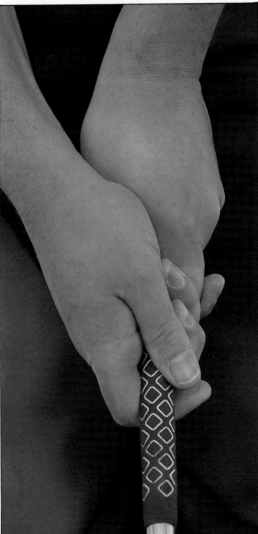

TOP LEFT The grip should be laid across the middle two fingers, as these need to have control of the shot.

ABOVE AND LEFT When closing the right hand, the left thumb is hidden. Both hands should grip the club with an even amount of pressure.

● THE VARDON GRIP ●

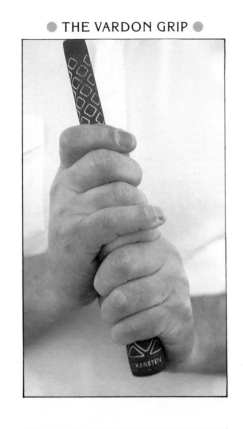

The little finger of the right hand rests on the forefinger of the left hand.

● THE INTERLOCK GRIP ●

The left hand takes the same role as before, but when the right hand closes over the club grip the little finger of the right hand interlocks with the forefinger of the left hand. Instead of merely overlapping it, it comes between the first two fingers of the left hand, thus locking the hands together.

There is one other acceptable grip if you find you cannot feel comfortable with the first two.

● THE DOUBLE-HANDED GRIP ●

Once again, the left hand takes the position on the club grip described before. To complete the grip, you bring in your right hand on to the club so that all four fingers of the right hand grip the club equally. The right thumb lies to the left of the club grip, completing a V pointing between the right-hand side of the head and the right shoulder. The palm of the right hand smothers the left thumb. It must be stressed that this grip encourages excessive use of the hands, and unless the hands are kept as close together as possible, shots will start to go astray.

The Vardon, or overlapping grip is recommended, but you must use the grip with which you are comfortable.

● COMMON FAULTS ●

Two faults are common when gripping the club. The first is called a 'strong grip' and occurs when one of the hands (usually the right) slips round to the right hand side of the grip. This takes the palm off its square line to the target, and the V of the hand is now running up the right arm.

The club-face, in addressing the ball, may appear square to the target, but the hands are not. When the ball is struck, the tension created in the arms will bring the hands square to the target line but the club-face will be twisted. In effect, the club-face will have been closed, sending the ball to the left.

The other common fault is the 'weak grip', which occurs when one of the hands (usually the left) slips round the left hand side of the grip. The back of the left hand is now off the target line, although the clubhead appears to be square. The V of the left hand will be running up the left arm. When the ball is struck, tension created in the arms will bring the hands square to the target line but, again, the club-face will be twisted. This time it will have been opened, and the result will be a wayward shot to the right.

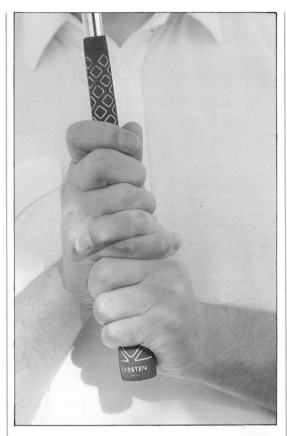

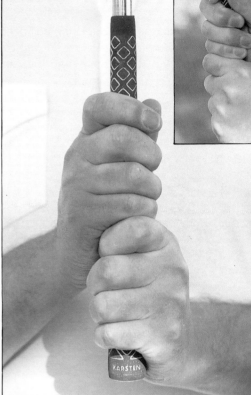

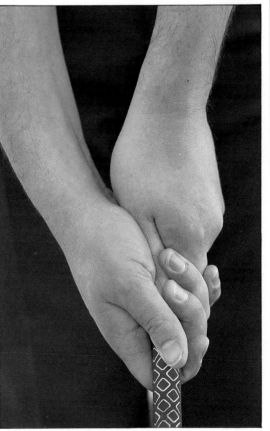

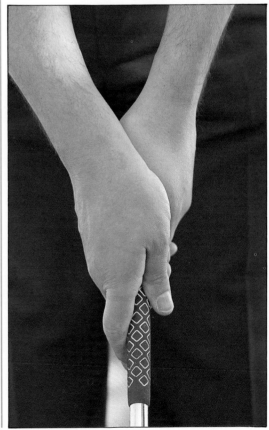

FAR LEFT *The interlocking grip:* the index finger of the left hand interlocks with the little finger of the right hand.

LEFT AND INSET ABOVE *The double-handed grip:* all eight fingers are on the club. When this grip is used, great care should be taken to keep the hands as close together as possible.

FAR LEFT *The strong grip:* the 'V' of either hand (usually the right), points to the right shoulder. When the ball is struck, the hand becomes square, which closes the club-face.

LEFT *The weak grip:* the 'V' formed by the thumb and forefinger points towards the left shoulder. When the ball is struck the hand becomes square and opens the club-face.

• THE STANCE •

The width between the feet at the stance is determined by the club chosen, which in turn depends on the type of shot to be played. The feet are closest together for the putting stroke, and they get farther apart as the shot gets longer, being at their widest for the drive.

Except for special awkward shots, the shoulders and hips should be square with the toes, which should be on a parallel line to the target line — or the 'railway track' as imagined when taking aim. The body weight will be evenly distributed between the feet.

The position of the stance in relation to the ball is also determined by the choice of club. There are two acceptable positions, the first favoured by beginners and the second by players with greater experience and confidence.

For beginners the address position varies through the range of shots from driver to wedge.

Because the ball needs to be struck on the upward swing path, the drive should be addressed in line with the left heel.

The address position then moves forward about an inch (25 mm) for every club needed until, when you use the wedge, because you need to strike the ball at the bottom of the down swing, the address is made with the ball in line with the mid-point of the space between the feet.

The second address position is for the more confident golfer and is the one favoured by most golf professionals. All the shots are played with the ball lying opposite the inside of the left heel. With this method the feet are close together for the wedge shot, and the stance widens gradually for shots using clubs going up the range. So the driver would be taken with the ball still lying opposite the left, heel, but the stance would have widened to shoulder width.

● BALL POSITION ●

When you take up the address position, the ball should be about an inch further forward for every club used, from the short-irons to the driver. The less loft on the club-face, the further forward the ball needs to be.

● THE ADDRESS POSITION ●

1 Stand up straight with the shoulders back, the head up and arms at your sides.

2 Keeping your back and legs straight, push your bottom out, bringing your head over towards the ball.

3 Keeping your back straight, relax the tension in your knees.

4 Now let your arms hang straight down, enabling you to swing your arms freely.

5 Grip the club; you are now in the address position.

● POSTURE ●

Your posture is your general bearing in the stance. Begin by imagining you are in the services and stand to attention. Stand straight, shoulders back and head up. Now bend over from the waist, keeping the back and legs straight. Push your bottom out and bend over one more notch. To release any tension, let your knees flex a little. Let your arms and hands hang down towards your left thigh, and grip the club. You are now in the address position.

● SHOT SAVER ●

When you are in the address position your hands should block your view of the shoe-laces of the left shoe. If they do not, step back and take up your position again.

ON THE GREEN
(RULES 8–2B, 16–1A)

You are not allowed to put any guide mark down on the green to help you find the target line. You can remove sand or loose soil between your ball and the hole by brushing it aside with your hand or club, but you must not press it down.

● LINING UP THE PUTT ●

1 Stand behind the ball and try to imagine the target line running from the ball to the hole.

2 After assuming a comfortable posture, your eyes should be positioned over the ball.

● THE SWING ●

Many novices embrace the full game of golf from pitch and putt courses where their appetite for golfing enjoyment has outpaced their ability. They wish to graduate to 18-hole courses to meet new challenges on manicured greens and trim fairways, which means learning the full swing.

Before you start the patient build-up of the swing, it will help if you understand its different components. Familiarity with the aim, grip, stance, the position of the ball and posture have already given you a basic technique on which you can build as you seek to swing the club. New ingredients will be added as you progress.

The golf swing is a circle designed by the hands, and described by the clubhead. The hands swing the club in an arc on the backswing, downswing and follow-through. These all form part of the same circle which is centred on the upper region of the chest. A putt is a small sector of a circle, with the clubhead making a small arc, but as the shots build up, your hands go further back until the arc increases to a circle – and you have formed your swing. Shots in the golf game which you are now about to play as you read begin with a winner – the short putt. This is a shot you need never leave home to practise. The short putt is as important a part of your game as a 250-yard (230-m) drive. Remember the old adage of the professionals: 'you drive for show but you putt for dough'.

● THE SHORT PUTT ●

No matter how you play on the fairway, it is your putt which wins the hole. There is no shot in golf where individuality is expressed as much as in the putt. But as in all golf shots, you need golfing disciplines. You have to follow the 'Golden Rules' of aim, grip, stance, position of ball and posture before you swing the club.

Start with a two-foot (60-cm) putt. This putt introduces you to the feel in your hands when the clubhead strikes the ball. The club needed is, of course, the putter, one of the most 'personal' clubs in the set. The putting stroke is a backwards and forwards movement, like a pendulum. For this two-foot (60-cm) putt, it will be three to four inches (75 to 100 mm) back and three to four inches (75 to 100 mm) through.

Let me introduce another maxim here: it is recognized that good golf, reduced to its simplest elements, means doing the same thing over and over again . . .

Stand behind the ball and try to imagine the target line running from the ball to the hole. Once that line is in your mind, walk to the side of the ball, taking aim, and place the head of the putter behind the ball, square to the target line. Assume your grip. Then settle into the stance, with the ball opposite the middle of the feet, which should be four to five inches (100 to 125 mm) apart. Now check the posture, get comfortable, position your head over the ball so that your eyes are directly above it. Your head has to remain steady over the ball throughout.

With such a short putt you will not need to look for the hole. Now start the pendulum, keeping your wrists firm but your arms relaxed, taking the clubhead back about three to four inches (75 to 100 mm). Make sure that the clubhead is not straying from the target line, then let the pendulum swing through gently, striking the ball in the middle of the clubhead on its forward movement, rolling the ball along the target line.

Repeat this shot until you can judge the pace and distance of the ball consistently. This is a part of golf you can practise on your carpet, rolling the ball up to an imaginary hole. It will give you confidence in the feel of the putter. Keep practising this two-foot (60-cm) putt until you are confident you can make it every time.

**LIFTING THE BALL
(RULES 16–1B, 20–1)**
If you want to clean the ball when you are on the green, you can; but remember to mark the position of your ball, or you will lose a stroke.

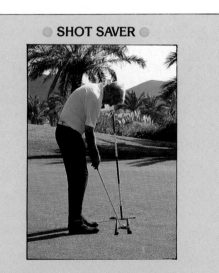

● SHOT SAVER ●

To sharpen your concentration, place two clubs parallel to the hole, one above the target line, the other below it. Putt through this corridor of confidence.

TESTING THE SURFACE (RULE 16–1D)

All of the rules of golf are simply a matter of common sense; when putting, it would of course be a great advantage to roll or tap a ball toward the hole before your putt, to test the borrow of the green and the quality of the surface, but doing so would negate so much of the challenge to your judgement and skill. Not surprisingly, it is against the rules.

● THE LONG PUTT ●

When you can putt out the two-footer (60 cm) regularly, start moving away from the hole until you reach the longer putt. Any putt from about 12 feet (3.5 m) to the edge of the green, can be called a long putt. With the longer putt, the striking power, which dictates the speed of the ball and therefore the distance it will travel, has to be practised to increase your confidence on the green. For the longer putts it does not matter if you do not hole out. The exercise is to try always to leave the ball 'dead' – so close that you can hole it next time. Do not forget: it is recognized that good golf, reduced to its simplest elements, means doing the same thing over and over again . . .

With the long putts, always look for the target line, then take your aim, grip and stance and make sure you keep your head still over the ball. Bring your clubhead back, keeping it square to the target line. Let the putter head strike the ball on its through swing, so that it rolls towards your target. The backswing and the follow-through will be about the same length. Both will become longer as the distance from the hole increases. Balance plays a very important part in the game of golf, and the general rule is that as the distance from the ball to the target increases, then your stance will have to widen. General tips about putting will be discussed later.

The long putt begins to involve a longer swing and is giving you more of the feel of the club as it strikes the ball. Fortunately, you need not play a full round or even one hole to refresh your putting confidence, as this can be practised indoors on a carpet. When you can rely on the putting stroke and your confidence has built up, move away from the green to get the feeling of the next shot in the build-up to the full swing.

This is going to be 40 yards (36 m) away from the target and you will use a club which for the first time will lift the ball off the ground, before it pitches and rolls on towards the target. This is a valuable shot made from just off the green, and is known as the 'chip and run'.

● THE CHIP AND RUN ●

The chip and run is, as its name suggests, two shots in one. The chip part of the shot forces the ball into the air. The run part is when the ball runs along the ground towards the hole, where you will be in a position to use one of your 'home-grown' putts that has been shaped and styled on your carpet.

For the chip and run you will need a 7-iron or an 8-iron. The loft on the club-face will chip the ball off the ground for the first part of its journey towards the target. Loft leads to lift. It is the clubhead striking the ball which lifts it into the air. You do not scoop the ball into the air with the clubhead; you let the loft on the club-face do the work. The swing action is the same as in putting, a pendulum, with the clubhead striking the ball as it swings through towards the target.

There is a 'new ingredient' to consider with this shot: head position. Your head has a heavy responsibility during the swing. It contributes one-eighth of your total body weight. It must not move until the ball has been struck and the clubhead is following through. Any slight movement of the head in any direction before this could have disastrous effects on your shot. After the clubhead has struck the ball your head will come up naturally, your eyes seeking the flight.

Stand behind the ball to picture the shot. Imagine you are going to throw the ball underarm towards the target. Picture its flight, and judge where it should land for the perfect result.

Do not attempt to hit the ball until you have had a few practice swings. This will help you visualize the shot. Take your address position, keeping your hands and wrists firm. For this practice exercise you are going to swing the club like a pendulum, as in the putting stroke. Keep your wrists firm (because you are going to make a wider arc), to take the clubhead back about two feet (60 cm) from the ball and two feet (60 cm) through it. Try to make this a crisp, positive action. Imagine that you can feel the clubhead sending the ball up and away towards the target. Let the turning of the left shoulder – to the right and away from the target – start the pendulum moving, keeping the left arm, hands, and golf club shaft all in a straight line. Your hands and wrists stay firm to ensure the clubface is square with the target line when it strikes the ball.

When you are happy with the method and confident with your practice shot, then you are ready to play the ball. Remember: it is recog-

● FAIRWAY CHIP AND RUN ●

Swing the club two feet back and two feet through, keeping your wrists firm and your head still, the ball should be in the middle of the feet. The outside edges of your feet should be a shoulder-width apart. The body weight should be evenly distributed and your hands in line with your left thigh, square to the target.

nized that good golf, reduced to its simplest elements, means doing the same thing over and over again . . .

Now take aim. Stand with the feet at right angles to the target line and ground the club-head behind the ball, square to the target line. Take your grip two inches (50 mm) from the top of the club grip. As you take up your stance the ball should be equidistant from your feet, with the outside of your shoes being a shoulder-width apart, and the body weight evenly distributed. Your posture should be comfortable, with your legs slightly flexed. Your hands should be opposite the left thigh and blocking your vision of the left shoe laces.

The right knee should be kept in the flexed address position throughout the shot. This is very important. Now swing the club – remembering the pendulum – two feet (60 cm) back and two feet (60 cm) through, letting the momentum of the clubhead strike the ball and lift it off the ground on its way to the target.

The chip and run to the green played correctly and cleanly must be one of the most rewarding shots in golf. Just as you did not rely entirely on being on a green to gain confidence in the putting action, you may now develop your rhythm for the chip and run shot by just swinging the club without hitting a ball.

You have discovered how loft on the club-face can lift the ball through the air with the chip and run shot. You are now beginning to build up the golf swing. The next stage is the half-swing, before you take the final instructions for the full swing. The half-swing will help to give you feel and rhythm. By varying the distance in practice, you will gain control over the flight of the ball.

● THE HALF-SWING ●

With the chip and run shot, your hands only went back a few inches. Now, with the half-swing, the hands are going to swing to waist height. The arc described by the hands in the backswing, downswing and follow-through, form part of the same circle, centred in the upper region of the chest. The arc gradually gets fuller as the distance of the shot increases. With the short putt, the hands only move back a few inches so the arc is very small. As you progress through the range of clubs to the full drive, the arc will increase to its maximum.

From the chip and run position, walk back up the fairway towards the tee. When you are about 90 yards (83 m) from the green you are in a position for a half-swing. The club required is a 6- or 7-iron. Imagine the ball is lying on the fairway.

There is another new ingredient for this shot: weight transference. An exercise to help you to understand the concept of weight transference is the simple one of throwing a ball underarm. Hold a ball in your right hand and face the target. Stand with your feet slightly apart, the weight even. Now take your arm back and let the weight move onto the right foot. Take a step forward with the left foot and gently swing your arm forward to release the ball. The weight is now on the left foot. Repeat this exercise a few times, then swing the club and be conscious of feeling your weight transferring from your right leg at the top of the half-swing, moving onto the left leg as you swing your arms through.

You are about 90 yards (83 m) from your target, so stand behind the ball to picture its flight. Work out your aim. Ground your clubhead behind the ball square to the target line. Form your grip, then assume your stance with the outer edges of your feet at shoulder-width. The hands should be four to five inches (100 to 125 mm) from the left thigh.

The right knee must stay in the flexed address position throughout the backswing. The left shoulder, arm, hand, club, as well as the left knee, all turn together, with the left arm pushing the golf club back and away from the target, to a position where the hands are at waist-height. The right hip moves backwards away from the ball. Your head stays steady, looking at the ball. Your posture will have remained at the same angle as at the address position. Your shoulders will have turned about 45°. At the top of the backswing, your hands will be waist-high, and

TRANSFER OF BODY WEIGHT

1 Throwing the ball underarm: a pointer to weight distribution. The weight transfers from the right leg to the left leg. This must be repeated in the golf swing, but without the head movement. Stand with your feet close together, facing the target with the ball in the right hand and body weight evenly distributed on both feet.

2 As the arm comes back, the weight transfers to the right leg.

3 The left leg steps forward, transferring the weight from the right to the left leg.

4 The ball has been released and the weight is on the right foot with the right heel off the ground.

● THE HALF-SWING ●

1 Stand behind the ball and picture the target line.

2 Take up the address position, with the club-head behind the ball, square to the target line.

3 The hands are waist-high, with the weight just on the inside of the right foot and the shoulders turned through 45°.

4 The hands have come through to waist height, the weight has transferred to the left leg and the head has not moved.

your weight will be just on the inside of your right foot.

The downswing starts with a lateral movement of the hips, the hands beginning to move at the same time. The force of the clubhead striking downwards transfers the body weight onto the left foot. The clubhead strikes through the ball on its path towards the target. The hands will finish waist-high. The half-swing has become a half circle. Let your right heel ease off the ground as your weight transfers.

Practise the half-swing until you can control the shot, before moving on to the full swing.

Remember my motto: it is recongized that good golf, reduced to its simplest elements, means doing the same thing over and over again . . .

No two players in the world have exactly the same full swing because of differences in height, build, age and fitness. Like the carpet putt which builds up confidence on the green, the half-swing can be practised anywhere, and without a ball, to build up confidence for tackling the full swing.

**THE SWING
(RULE 13–2)**
You cannot remove obstructions to your swing, such as grass or branches, or anything marking the area which is out of bounds such as a fence post or wire. It is alright to touch these obstructions in the backswing, so that you can, for example, push the club back through long grass.

⬤ THE FULL SWING ⬤

There is a whole recipe of ingredients needed for the full swing: aim, grip, stance, posture, swing, weight transference, wrist cock, body turn and swing plane.

Wrist cock is a new ingredient. It is an integral part of the back-swing and should not be cultivated as an independent action. The weight of the clubhead, provided the grip is correct, allows the wrists to cock naturally throughout the back swing. Here is an exercise to give you the feel of the wrist cock, an action which will accelerate the clubhead in the shot. Stand straight, feet slightly apart for balance. Grip the club correctly. Lift up the club, pointing it away from you at shoulder height, with your arms fully outstretched and the shaft of the club parallel to the ground. Keeping your arms straight, 'break' the wrists so that the club shaft points vertically upwards. Turn the shoulders 90° to the right. This is the feel of a wrist cock.

Body turn is another new ingredient – and note it is body turn and *not* body sway. An exercise to give you the feel of the body turning also doubles as a second exercise to give you the feeling of wrist cock. The movement is similar in style to that of a baseball player when striking a ball. Select any golf club, form the grip with your hands, and stand up straight, with your arms stretched out in front of you parallel to the ground. The head remains in the central position. Let your knees bend slightly. The right knee must stay in the bent address position throughout the first part of the turn.

Now let your left shoulder lead the turn of your left side to the right, keeping your left arm firm and turning the shoulders through a full 90°. Your hips will have turned 45° if your right knee has stayed in the bent position as at the address. Your arms will have rotated like the hands of a clock. The back of the left hand will be facing upwards, as will the palm of the right. The right arm will have bent, with the elbow pointing down to the ground. The left knee will have bent in and pushed forward slightly, pointing to a spot about twelve inches (30 cm) behind the ball. This will have helped the weight to transfer onto the right leg and your right side.

Keeping your gripped hands parallel to the ground, you start the turn in the opposite direction to the left, drawn by a slight lateral movement of the hips. Your arms move anti-clockwise, unwinding the movement. When your body is facing the left, your hands will have naturally

● WRIST BREAK IN THE BACKSWING ●

1 Stand straight. Grip the club correctly with your arms fully outstretched at shoulder height and the shaft of the club parallel to the ground.

2 Keeping your arms straight, break the wrists so that the club shaft points vertically upwards.

3 Turn the shoulders through 90° to the right. This gives the feel of the wrist-cock at the top of the backswing.

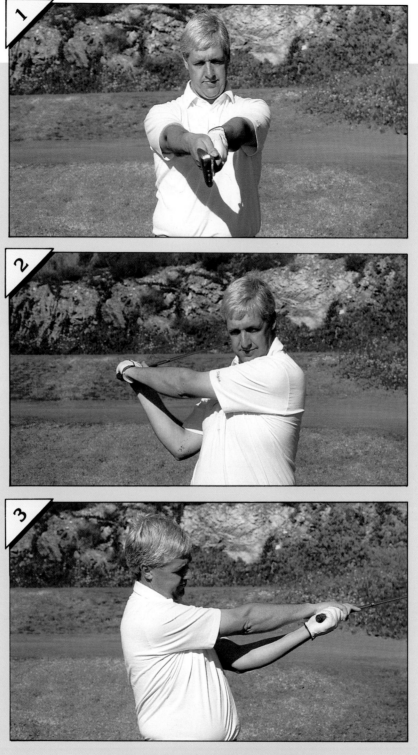

● BODY TURNING EXERCISE ●

1 Stand straight, with your arms outstretched and the club parallel to the ground.

2 Turn the left shoulder to the right through 90°, which will automatically turn the hips through 45°. The back of the left hand points upwards, the back of the right points downwards.

3 Turn the shoulders in the opposite direction so that the right shoulder turns to the left. The back of the right hand now points upwards and the back of the left points downwards.

rotated in an anti-clockwise direction, so that the back of the right hand and palm of the left hand face the sky. The right arm will be straight, the left arm bent, with the elbow pointing straight down.

Repeat this body turning movement several times, feeling your weight transferring from one leg to the other. You will discover that the transfer is governed by the position of your hands. Your weight transfers as your hands move from the backswing to the follow-through. You will achieve a natural wrist cock, or break, at each end of this lateral arm movement, which will be used in the full swing exercises.

The third new ingredient in the full swing is the plane. The plane is the angle of the circle of the swing shaped by the hands as they move the club around the body. The posture which creates this is determined by the club needed to play the shot. The wedge and the driver mark the two opposite ends of the spectrum, which give an upright and a flat plane respectively. The shaft of the wedge is shorter and the lie angle more upright. This forces the player to stand nearer the ball and take a more upright stance. And because of this, the swing will follow a more upright plane. The driver, with the longest shaft in the bag and the flattest lie, forces the player into a flatter swing plane.

Many mechanical devices have been produced down the years to perfect a personalized swing for the learner golfer. Some eccentric home-grown ideas are now prize relics in golfing museums. Golf is one sport where new technology is always waiting to help. A warm welcome is now being given to the golf 'Swing Simulator', which personalizes swings for golfers of all heights and physiques. It gives a constant plane and operates on muscle memory.

With or without the help of a swing simulator, you are now ready to practise the full swing.

You have learnt that the golf swing is a circle defined by the hands, with the chest being the centre of the circle. It is important that the distance between the hands and the chest remain as near constant as possible throughout the swing. This is popularly known as 'keeping the left arm firm'. A swing must travel full circle, taking the ball with it along its perfect path.

Select a middle iron for this shot, a 5-iron or 6-iron. After lining up your shot and taking aim, form your grip and assume your stance. Your feet are a little wider apart than for the half-swing on which this full swing is built. The middle of

MOVABLE OBSTRUCTIONS (RULE 24–1)

What happens in the rare event that your ball comes to rest against someone's golf bag or rolls under a golf cart? An obstruction is defined as anything artificial (except objects marking out of bounds). If the obstruction can be moved without disturbing the ball, go ahead. If not, and you are not on the tee or the green, you will have to drop the ball: hold the ball at shoulder height and arm's length to do this.

LEFT Most of the time you will be aiming to strike the ball squarely with the club-face and therefore the stance you adopt should be square to the line of the shot, as shown. If the clubhead remains on line to the flag from the top of the backswing, through the ball and to the top of the follow-through, just before the wrist break, then you will have achieved a *direct swing path*. You should be able to feel through the grip that the clubhead is working on a straight line.

● THE GOLF SWING SIMULATOR ●

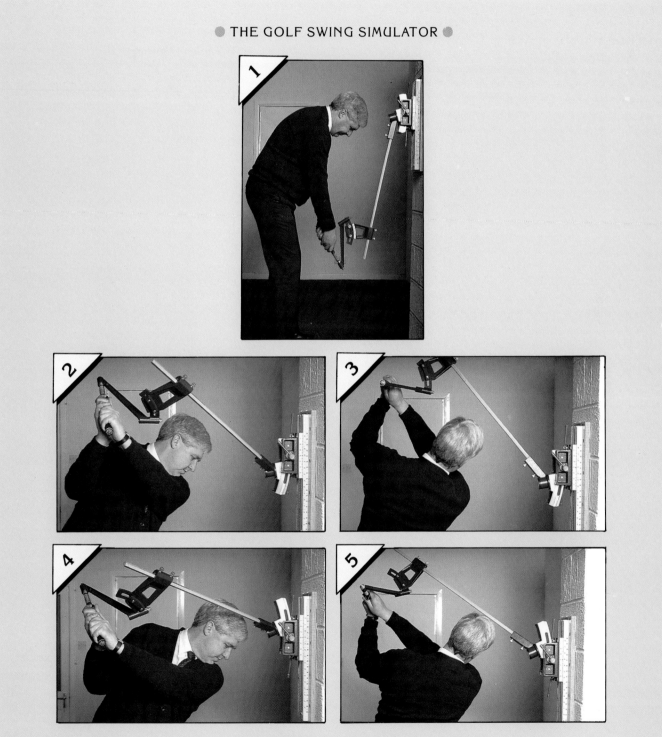

The golf Swing Simulator can be adjusted for the full range of planes, from flat to upright. 1, 2 and 3 show a setting for a more upright plane than 4 and 5.

● THE FULL SWING ●

1 The posture must remain the same until the ball is struck.

2 Select a five-iron and take up your address position.

each foot should now line up with your shoulders. Your club is square to the ball. Recall the importance of the target-line. Remember to keep the posture the same throughout the swing. The right knee remains flexed. Allow the left knee to bend naturally, as with the half-swing, when the left shoulder turns and the left arm pushes the hands, shaft and clubhead back away from the ball.

From about waist-high the arms will start moving clockwise – as in the baseball exercise – and the wrists will start cocking. The backswing follows a constant plane. The hands reach the height of the right shoulder. The shoulders are turned through 90°. The hips have now turned 45°. The weight has transferred to the instep of the right foot. It is acceptable for the left heel to have lifted slightly off the ground. As the wrists break during the backswing, the club shaft is pointing towards the target and the club-face is square to the plane. The right thumb is under the shaft. The right elbow is pointing straight down behind the line of the heel. The left knee points to a spot 12 inches (30 cm) behind the ball. The downswing and follow-through complete the full swing, as the clubhead goes

3 Push the club back to waist height before beginning the wrist cocking procedure.

4 At the top of the backswing, the club shaft is in line with the target. The left arm is firm and the right elbow points to the ground, behind the heel line.

through the ball, sweeping it towards its target.

The enemy of accuracy in this part of the full swing is body sway, which can be generated too easily by the momentum of the arms and hands coming through as the body weight transfers. If you keep your body posture the same throughout the swing, it will prevent the temptation to sway. The hands and the lateral movement of the hips initiate the downswing, and the force of the clubhead striking downwards unlocks the wrists, as the hands and arms sweep on smoothly through the ball to the high finish of the swing. Keep your eye behind the ball as you strike it. The hips have turned, to bring the front of the body to face the target. Your right shoulder will have pushed your chin up.

The body weight follows your hands. It moves from the right foot and left instep at the top of the backswing, through to the left foot at the finish of the swing. The sole of the right shoe will be off the ground and pointing away from the target, and your knees will be close together. This follow-through gives power and flight to your shot. Finish high and let it fly! Remember that when you throw a ball underhand, you get no height or flight unless you follow through.

● CLUB POSITION AT THE TOP OF THE BACKSWING ●

1 The club-face is square, with the club shaft pointing towards the target. From this position, there is a good chance the ball will be on target.

2 The club is pointing across the target, resulting in an out-to-in swing which lends slice-spin to the ball, making it go left in a straight line or on a slice trajectory.

3 From this position, an in-to-out swing will result in the ball going either right in a straight line, or hooking around to the left.

● POSITIONING THE RIGHT HAND ●

1 Positioning the right hand at the top of the backswing. Swing the club to the top of the backswing, with the shaft pointing towards the target.

2 The right elbow must point straight down behind the right heel. The shaft is parallel with the ground.

3 Swing the right arm through until your arm is level with your shoulder. You must keep your head still throughout and keep looking at the ball.

APPLYING YOUR SKILLS

Once you have established the basic principles of striking the ball with reasonable control and accuracy, you must adapt your technique to the demands of the golf course. You must review and refine your shots to meet the different challenges you will meet from tee to green.

You are now familiar with the rudiments of the golf swing. You know the importance of the disciplines of taking aim and lining up your clubhead square, after establishing a target line for each shot. You should follow them as naturally as you look both ways before crossing a busy road.

Now is the time to analyze all stages of your game from tee to green. As before, the best way to start is to sharpen your skills in the short game around the greens. Then you can move back down the fairway towards the tee. As you go, you can take a second look at the structure of every important shot. You will learn to take more than one look before every shot. You will appreciate again my motif: it is recognized that good golf, reduced to its simplest elements, means doing the same thing over and over again . . .

● FOUR-FOOT PUTT ●

1 When lining-up a putt to help you judge the distance, stand behind the ball and imagine rolling the ball towards the hole. This will help to get the strength right when making the putt.

2 You must take great care in lining up the face of the putter with the hole.

3 Make sure your eyes are over the ball when assuming the address position.

4 A smooth putting stroke must be in your mind when you take the clubhead back.

5 Keep your wrists firm as your putter head goes through to roll the ball towards the hole.

● PUTTING ●

Putting is a pressure shot in golf. It can be the most exciting. In the televised international golf tournaments which make heroes for the more modest golfer to emulate, it is the greens which are the arenas of drama, and the shot which excites both the armchair spectators and the crowd on the course, is the putt which drops.

When you are facing any putt, short or long, do not trust to luck. Watch the care the top players take with even the simpler looking putts. See how they go through the routine of seeking the target line, taking aim, assuming stance – and how they achieve steadiness. You too can become a master of the green.

To putt well, it will help if you understand a little about the construction of a green. Flat greens are optical illusions. Golf course architects cannot build them. The necessary drainage requires greens to have a high and low point. So there must be a slope, which in golf is called a borrow. Often you have to aim off-line to compensate for the slope or borrow. When on the green, look for these high and low spots which will affect your putt. Because of the way greens are cut, the amount of slope on a green can be disguised.

Your putter can be a useful plumb line in assessing the borrow and in finding the target line. Stand behind the ball, lining it up with the hole. Hold the putter out in front of you, thumb and first finger on the grip, shaft pointing vertically downwards and blade pointing out towards the hole for balance. From behind the ball, with one eye closed, line up the straight side of the shaft with the side of the ball and the hole in your vision. You are using the hanging shaft as a plumb line. It will give you an idea of the borrow between the ball and the hole, and how much you need to allow in your putt for the ball to swing in towards the hole.

From anywhere on the putting green – and greens come in a wide range of sizes – your hope is to hole out with one putt. But to take the pressure off the long putts, modify your objective a little. Try to roll the ball close to the hole. Your primary objective is to lay your putt dead, just a tap away from the hole. Your putting standard will improve if you weigh up the length of the grass on the green. If it has been cut that day, the pace will be faster. The way the nap lies will affect speed and borrow.

Every shot calls for concentration and smooth movement. Remember that each hole on the course is precisely 4¼ inches (107.95 mm) in diameter. Putting is no pushover. It breeds in some players unbelievable reliance upon a particular design or weight of putter and leads to extraordinary idiosyncracies in style, stance and grip. But you should try to putt accurately with the orthodox methods, although your grip may change slightly as you progress.

One rule in putting is never to let the clubhead pass your hands. This common fault arises when you try to anticipate the strike, causing the wrists to flick or break just before the ball is struck. To stop this happening, many players use an alternative grip known as the 'reverse overlap'. With this method the left hand is on the putter grip, with the thumb going straight down the grip. When the right hand is placed in position, the forefinger of the left hand covers the two smallest fingers of the right. The thumb of the right hand also points straight down the shaft. The overlapping forefinger helps keep the arm, wrist, hand and finger all in one line, firming up the wrist. It also keeps the two hands close together, making them work as one unit.

The putt is the only stroke in which you should move away from the orthodox grip. Another, used to great effect by the German champion, Bernard Langer, is the 'cackhanded' grip. For this you place the left hand in a line below the right. This keeps the arms, wrist and hands moving as one unit. It is in some ways a left-handed golfer's grip, used by a right-hander.

Some players favour their trusted putter for short shots from off the green in preference to chipping. This shot has been dubbed the 'Texas Wedge'.

Putting's golden rules are that your eyes must be over the ball and your head must be still throughout the putting stroke. Your whole body should resemble a statue, except for a smooth movement from your arms and shoulders.

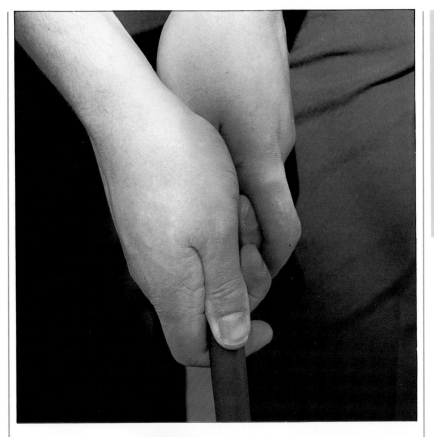

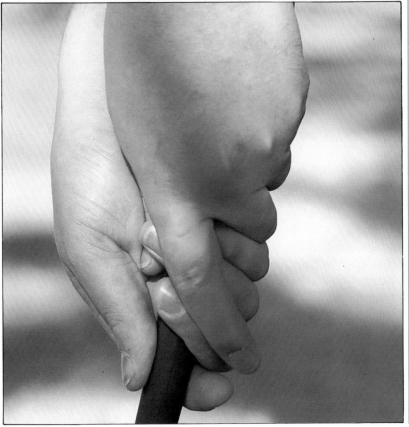

● **SHOT SAVER** ●

Before playing a round, check whether your eyes are directly over the ball in your putting stance with a novel test you can carry out on the practice green. Line up for a putt, then hold a spare ball to the bridge of your nose, between your eyes. Let the ball drop. If it hits the one you have lined up, you know your eyes are not going to let you down. If it misses, reposition your head until you get it right. This will boost your confidence for the putts out on the course.

ABOVE The golden rules of putting are that your eyes must be over the ball at the address position and that your head must be kept still throughout the stroke.

● PITCHING AND CHIPPING ●

Around the green you will be faced with a variety of shots which demand either short, high flights to leap hazards, or low flighted runs to the hole. The first shot is a pitch, the second a chip. Where you cannot use a putter, a chip is safer than a pitch. As a famous player once said: 'With all greenside shots, always try to make the ball land as near as possible to you.' The point is that, as a general rule, it is easier to judge run than flight; although the speed of the greens is an important factor in deciding which route to take to the hole.

The pitch and chip shots are the foundations of an accurate short game. The loft of the club does the work for both. The pitch will be played with the more lofted club, the chip played with the straighter face.

ABOVE To see the result of your putt, *turn* your head to follow the ball's path to the hole. Do not lift your head to watch the ball.

● THE PITCH ●

A typical pitch shot is the one needed to clear a bunker which guards a green. Stand behind the ball and visualize just where you wish the ball to land, and its flight. Face the hole and swing your arm backwards and forwards, giving you the feel of the shot. Imagine for a moment that you were going to throw the ball. The follow-through would be longer than the backswing. This is also true of your pitch shot. Remembering this will help ensure that you don't stop on the shot: think of it as one-third back and two-thirds through.

In the early stages, it is advisable to play to the widest part of the green for safety. This will make for an easier shot. One thing you do not wish to do is to take your next shot from deep in the bunker. Even tournament professionals do not always aim for the pin, but play 'percentage shots', those which offer the greater percentage chance of success in the end.

Now you have the flight in your mind, select your club and study the lie. You may be tempted to loft the ball with the sand wedge, because that has the greatest loft of all the clubs in the bag. The danger is that if the ball is not cushioned by the grass, the heavy flange of the sand wedge will work against you. The ideal club for a pitch must therefore be the pitching wedge.

For the high pitch shot, assume a stance that positions the ball nearer to the left, or front, foot, forward of the centre line between your feet. Your feet should be fairly close together, the out-sides of your feet no wider than your shoulders. Your weight will be slightly more on your left side, with your knees relaxed. This cuts down the transference of weight when you swing the club and helps to keep the body still. This in turn helps you to hit down and through the ball.

With this shot, a slight amount of wrist break is necessary to steepen the clubhead on the downswing, and give a little extra clubhead speed into the ball. When striking the ball, the blade of the club, coming down under the ball, will lift it up and over the bunker to the green. Remember to follow through to ensure you don't 'quit' through the ball. Let the loft of the club do the work. Do not try to scoop. If you do, you are likely to find yourself in the bunker.

The length of your follow-through will be determined by the distance you wish the ball to pitch on the green — and remember you are not relying on much run.

LEFT To pitch a shot, use a lofted club to help give more lift to the ball.

BELOW LEFT To chip a shot, use a straighter faced club. The ball will stay closer to the ground and will have more run.

DIFFERENT ABILITIES

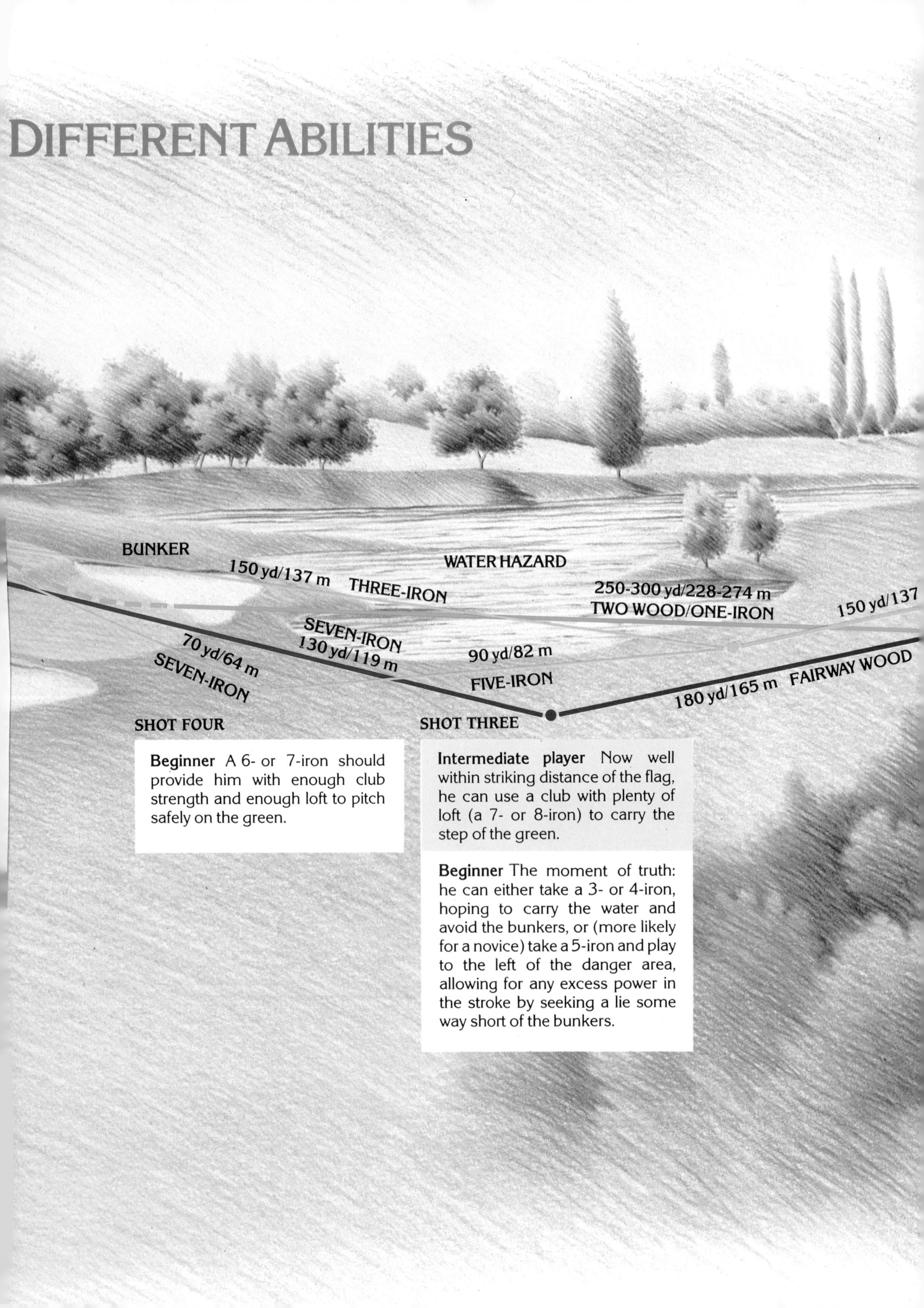

BUNKER

150 yd/137 m   THREE-IRON

WATER HAZARD

250-300 yd/228-274 m
TWO WOOD/ONE-IRON

150 yd/137

SEVEN-IRON
130 yd/119 m

70 yd/64 m
SEVEN-IRON

90 yd/82 m

FIVE-IRON

180 yd/165 m   FAIRWAY WOOD

SHOT FOUR

SHOT THREE

Beginner A 6- or 7-iron should provide him with enough club strength and enough loft to pitch safely on the green.

Intermediate player Now well within striking distance of the flag, he can use a club with plenty of loft (a 7- or 8-iron) to carry the step of the green.

Beginner The moment of truth: he can either take a 3- or 4-iron, hoping to carry the water and avoid the bunkers, or (more likely for a novice) take a 5-iron and play to the left of the danger area, allowing for any excess power in the stroke by seeking a lie some way short of the bunkers.

PLAYING A PAR FIVE
DIFFERENT SOLUTIONS FOR PLAYERS OF

The very fact that a system of handicapping (first officially introduced in 1926) is used in golf will tell you that the approach to each of the challenges posed by any hole is — and should be — different for players of different standards. The illustration shows the routes taken to the green by three golfers of varying abilities and experience. All three, in effect, play an ideal game from tee to green, according to their own capabilities.

BACK BUNKER

TIERED GREE

BUNKER

● FADE ●

The clubhead is swung on an out-to-in path, with the club-face open from that path; the ball is faded from left to right.

● THE PITCH SHOT ●

1 A pitch shot is often necessary to clear a bunker. Stand behind the ball and visualise the flight you would like the ball to take.

2 The ball must be closer to the left foot than the right. Keep your feet fairly close together.

● SHOT SAVER ●

If you decide to putt from off the green imagine the hole not as a drainpipe but as big as a manhole cover. It would be a huge stroke of luck to hole from such a distance. But by using your imagination like this you could be encouraged to put the ball close enough to hole out next time.

If you take a mid-iron for chipping, the ball does not need to be struck so forcefully because of the lesser loft of the club.

Imagine the shot, face the hole and swing the arm — one third back and two-thirds through. You must not fluff this shot by hitting the ground before the ball. So whereas the width of your stance should be the same as for the pitch, inside a shoulder-width, the ball should be positioned opposite the middle of the space between your feet. Your hands should be opposite your left thigh, with your weight over your left foot. The weight stays there throughout the shot and the only movement is from the arms and shoulders. Your head stays still over the ball.

Because there is no wrist break needed for this shot, the position of your hands assumes even more importance. As you play through the shot, keep the same angle of hands to clubhead; do not let the clubhead fly through because of floppy wrists. There is no place for wrist flicks in golf.

● THE FAIRWAY WOOD ●

1 Stand behind the ball to picture the shot.

2 The ball should be towards the left heel as you take up your stance.

3 Push the club back, keeping the arc wide.

LEFT For the mid-iron shot, the stance should be a little wider than for the short-irons. The ball should be between the left heel and the middle of the feet.

ABOVE When playing a mid-iron, keep the swing under control and do not over-swing. The club-face should be square to the plane and the shaft of the club pointing on-line to the target.

3 A slight amount of wrist break is necessary in the back-swing, to steepen the arc on the down-swing.

4 The length of the follow-through is determined by how far ahead you wish the ball to pitch onto the green. Let the loft of the club do the work. Do not try to scoop the ball.

● THE CHIP ●

The chip gives run to the ball and is used for equally short approaches to the green as the pitch, being preferred where there are no trouble spots to fly over. It is played with a straighter-faced club, like a mid-iron.

Before considering your chip, ask yourself if your putter, used as a 'Texas Wedge', might be more successful. If you were, say, 12 feet (4 m) off the green with 45 feet (14 m) of green to the hole and, using the putter, swept the ball towards the hole so that it stopped 6 feet (2 m) from it, you might feel disappointed. But if you got to the same spot by chipping, you could feel pleased. Your expectations are greater with a putter.

● SHORT IRON PLAY ●

The short iron is played for accuracy and not length. With the 7-iron, 8-iron and 9-iron the ball should be struck from just forward of the middle of your feet, with your hands opposite the left thigh covering your view of the left shoelace. Your body weight should be evenly distributed and your knees slightly flexed. Your feet should be slightly closer together than a shoulder-width. Take a three-quarter backswing. Because of the position of the ball, the clubhead will strike down slightly into the ground, taking a shallow divot, as the hands complete the arc through the ball to the top of the follow-through.

You will find greater consistency if you take a stronger club than you think you need. Do not force your shot. You will be more consistent with

SHOT ONE

● Professional or scratch golfer ●
In order to reach the green in two shots, the professional uses the driver and closes his shoulders to impart a degree of hook spin, drawing the ball around the trees from right to left. (See illustration A.)

● Intermediate player ●
Without the control necessary to draw the ball around the trees, he uses the driver to gain maximum distance straight down the fairway, allowing himself plenty of room at the turn to avoid the copse with his second shot.

● Beginner ●
From the front tee position (which can be as much as 50 yards in front of the professional's competition tee) he might take a 2 or 3 wood instead of the driver, for greater control and confidence, happy to clear the stream and delighted to reach the turn of the dogleg.

Beginner

TEEING GROUND

● Intermediate Player

Professional

● Club Selection ●

Distance (yardage) and probable club used for each shot from tee to green.

Professional

250-300 yd/driver
250-300 yd/2 or 3 wood or 1-iron.

Intermediate Player

180-200 yd/driver
180-200 yd/3 or 4 wood
120-140 yd/7-iron.

Beginner

125-175 yd/2 or 3 wood
125-175 yd/2 or 3 wood or 3-iron
125-150 yd/3-iron or
80-100 yd/5-iron and 60-80 yd/6- or 7-iron

● DRAW ●
The clubhead is swung on an in-to-out path and the club-face closes from that path; the ball is drawn from right to left.

LEFT The ball position for the seven-, eight- and nine-irons should be opposite the middle of your feet with the hands in line with the left thigh.

BELOW LEFT The short-irons are used for accuracy. The length of the backswing is not as important as with the longer shots. Make sure that your backswing is compact. The most important objective is to ensure that your clubhead is on-line.

a stronger club and a shorter, but firmer swing. Let the clubhead do the work, and fight the temptation to scoop the ball.

The shorter irons give height to the flight of the ball, due to the shape of the club and the steeper arc and plane from which the ball is struck. These impart back spin to the ball; when it pitches on the green, very little run will occur.

● MID IRON PLAY ●

The 5-iron and 6-iron have shafts which are a little longer than the short distance irons and are therefore slightly more difficult to use.

To use them, your feet should be a little wider than for the short irons. Strike the ball from opposite a point between your left heel and the middle of your feet. When you stand behind the ball looking down towards the target and seeking the target line, imagine a corridor the width of the green you are playing towards. Try to flight the ball down that corridor. The length is not as important at this stage of the game as accuracy. The ball can always run on. The backswing need be only three-quarters of the full swing. When coming down and through the ball, take very little divot.

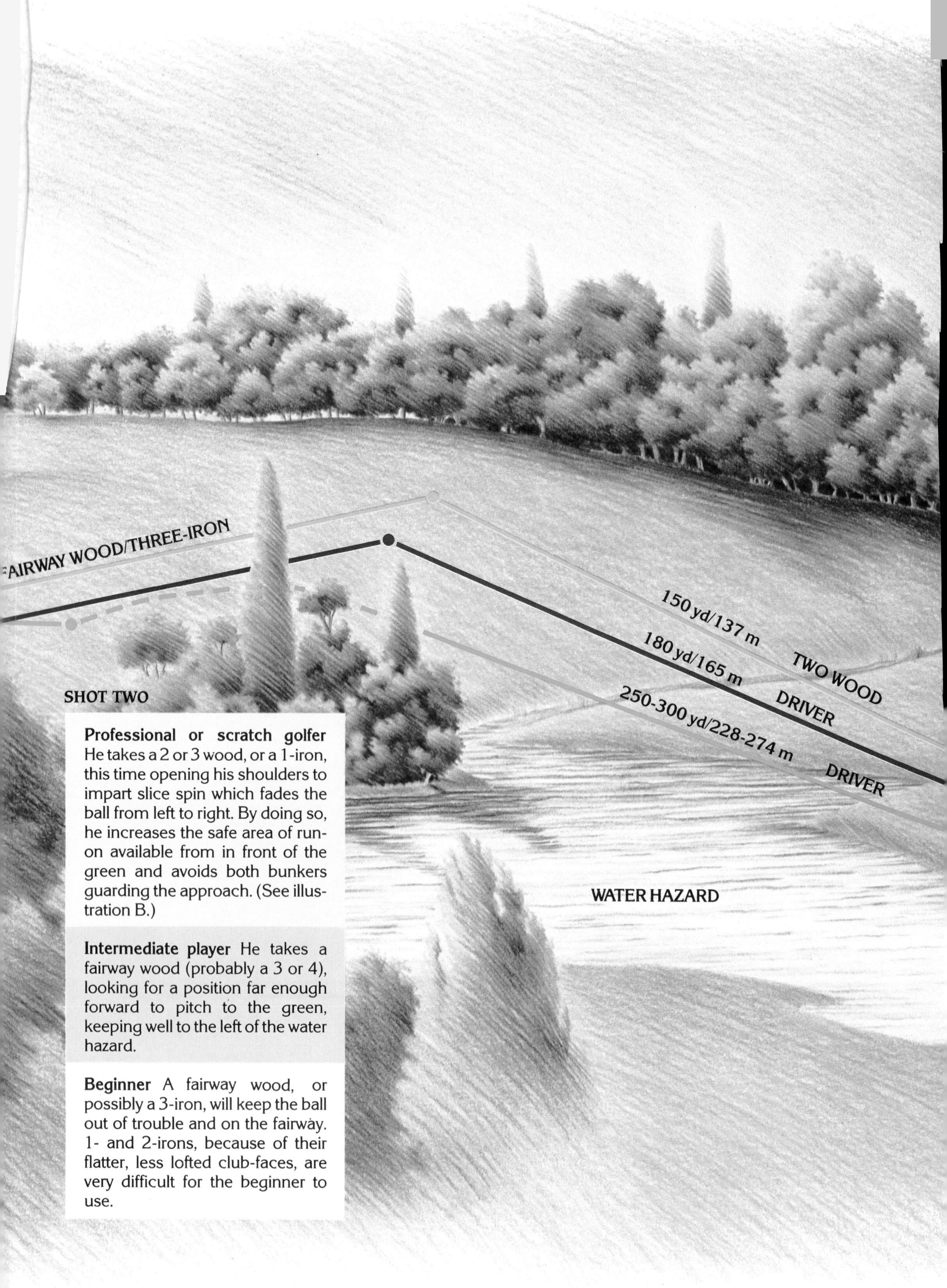

FAIRWAY WOOD/THREE-IRON

150 yd/137 m   TWO WOOD

180 yd/165 m   DRIVER

250-300 yd/228-274 m

DRIVER

WATER HAZARD

SHOT TWO

Professional or scratch golfer
He takes a 2 or 3 wood, or a 1-iron, this time opening his shoulders to impart slice spin which fades the ball from left to right. By doing so, he increases the safe area of run-on available from in front of the green and avoids both bunkers guarding the approach. (See illustration B.)

Intermediate player He takes a fairway wood (probably a 3 or 4), looking for a position far enough forward to pitch to the green, keeping well to the left of the water hazard.

Beginner A fairway wood, or possibly a 3-iron, will keep the ball out of trouble and on the fairway. 1- and 2-irons, because of their flatter, less lofted club-faces, are very difficult for the beginner to use.

● LONG IRON PLAY ●

The shafts of the 3-iron and 4-iron are even longer than those of the mid irons and the concept of swing plane discussed in the previous chapter comes into play. The lie angle of these irons is a little flatter than that of the others, and you will need to stand slightly farther away from the ball. This will flatten your plane and help you to sweep the ball forwards. Beginners should not be too ambitious in trying to carry this shot all the way to the green from the fairway. Look for the corridor towards the green as for the mid irons.

The feet should be wider apart with these irons than with the others, and the ball position should be further forward, towards the left heel than when using the mid irons. You should not take a divot, and the positioning of the ball towards the left foot will help. Swing and sweep it away off the turf down the 'corridor of confidence' you have set for yourself.

Be careful not to snatch this shot. Build confidence in your backswing to let your body turn and take your body weight through the shot, as it follows your hands.

PROVISIONAL BALL (RULE 27–2)
If one of your long iron shots were to go astray and there was a possibility of the ball being lost or out of bounds, it would be tedious to trudge down the course looking for it, only to have to return to the original lie to play a second ball. The rules allow you to play a provisional ball from as close as possible to the original position *before* you go forward to search. When you reach the area where the first ball came to rest, if you find it, then no penalty is incurred and the provisional ball doesn't count. If the first ball is lost, then carry on with the second, losing a stroke as normal.

4 At the top of the backswing, the shoulders should be turned through 90° and the club on-line with the target.

5 Strike through the ball with the correct weight transference. A good finish is essential.

RIGHT Note the differences between the driver and the fairway wood; the latter has a shorter shaft, a lighter clubhead, and greater loft. The shallowness of the head means its centre of gravity is below the ball, which assists in lifting the ball into the air.

LEFT The straighter face of the driver clubhead makes the shot more difficult to control than the shallower and more lofted face of the three wood.

RIGHT The height of the tee-peg plays a very important part in driving. The ball should be positioned opposite the left heel, with half the ball above the centre of the face and the other half below. The ball is swept away as the club starts its upward climb from the bottom of the arc towards the top of the follow-through.

● DRIVING ●

The drive, taken from the tee, is the most power-ful shot in golf, and can be the biggest trouble finder. It is usually played with the No. 1 wood, but if confidence in your swing is lacking there is no disgrace in taking a 3-wood. Although you are setting up your stance and swing to get the maximum distance with the ball, your main ob-jective is to find the fairway with the shot. The penalty of missing the fairway and finishing up in the rough – in Indian country – or out of bounds, can be disappointingly harsh. So don't gamble with the driver. Play the percentage shot from the tee: try to place your ball down the fairway in a spot where your lie for the next shot is clean, even if you are sacrificing some distance.

The height of the tee peg for the drive is important. Whichever wood you take to drive, you will find the height of the tee peg must rule the position of the ball as you set up your shot. You know that the golf swing is a circle and that the middle of the feet is the bottom of the arc. Therefore the higher you peg up, the further for-ward the ball should be positioned from the centre of your feet. If you tee up the ball on a high peg in the centre of the feet, the driver would sweep under the ball, making it fly off the top of the clubhead.

To use the driver your feet should be at their widest in the stance, the insides of your feet being as wide as your shoulders. As the numbers of the woods increase, so the stance on the tee narrows slightly.

The ideal spot to position the ball for the drive is to tee it up just inside the left foot. This will mean your head is slightly behind the ball. Half the ball should be above the club-face as it sits square on the ground behind it. As you swing into the ball this position allows your body weight to come through, achieving maximum power through your hands, arms and turning shoulders. The ball should then be smack in the middle of the club-face. Keep your head still. Do not let it drift in front of the ball, or that circle swing will loop you into trouble.

Once you have decided to take your driver, you should be totally committed to that shot. Take care to take a full body-turn away from the ball so that you may come back into the ball with a confident, smooth swing and the power to send it out on its way towards the target. And so watch that head. Keep it behind the ball.

LEFT The driver should be positioned just inside the left foot. The feet are a shoulder-width apart.

BELOW The ball is opposite the inside of the left foot and the clubhead is square to the target line.

● THE DRIVE ●

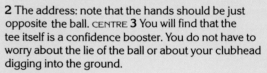

1 The correct alignment of head, feet, club-face and hands during the drive: look for the target line.

2 The address: note that the hands should be just opposite the ball. CENTRE **3** You will find that the tee itself is a confidence booster. You do not have to worry about the lie of the ball or about your clubhead digging into the ground.

● TEMPO ●

For a full-blooded shot like the drive, the tempo of the shot is important. For the backswing you should take the clubhead back slowly, brushing the ground, until it naturally lifts. The arc builds up and the wrists break at waist-height. Then you make the downward sweep into, and through, the ball.

No high-tech meter can measure and pro-gramme your individual tempo. Mature club golfers carry their own built-in ideas to regulate the tempo of their swing in the full shots. Until practice boosts your confidence a mental trick or two might be useful. Some players seeking self confidence softly hum the opening bars of the main musical theme of the Blue Danube waltz to themselves as they form the swing arc and follow through. It seems to have the right tempo. If it works for you: keep humming. A good drive, after all, is music to your ears.

4 Your left side becomes firm while your right leg and right side bend as you come up onto the toes of your right foot.

5 The club comes to rest almost diagonally across your shoulders.

● SHOT SAVER ●

A tip I learned years ago came from a veteran Scottish professional golfer, who was asked how to improve the tempo of those big hits off the tee. His dour reply was 'Alexander Cadogan'. I've forgotten who that professional was, but I pass on his tip. Just think of that name as you take the clubhead back slowly ... 'Alexander' ... and down the clubhead swoops through the circle of the arc and out again ... 'Cadogan' ..., the ball being struck on the middle syllable. The rhythm of the syllables is so similar to the different pace of the backswing and follow-through.

OFF THE FAIRWAY

You won't be on the fairway for all of your golfing life: this section will help you to understand the causes of wayward shots and what to do when faced with an awkward lie.

Golf shots fly off-line for many reasons. The fault may be in your own hands, your stance, your head position, swing, aim or balance. To identify typical faults you must first understand the concepts of target line and swing line. The target line runs from the ball to the target. That is the line which you take when lining up your shot. The swing line is the actual line taken by the clubhead as it goes from the backswing down into the ball and through to your finish.

If the clubhead goes back and then through on the same line, then it is in plane. If, however, from the top of the backswing you are in an upright position and at the finish of the shot you are in a flat position then you will have swung out of plane, on an out-to-in swing line. The opposite occurs when your hands at the top of the backswing are in a flat position and at the finish of the follow-through have moved into an upright position – then you have swung from in-to-out.

● CAUSES OF BAD SHOTS ●

The causes of bad shots are easiest explained in terms of table tennis. In this game slices and spins are exaggerated and intentional, and the effects easier to see than in golf.

● THE SLICE ●

The slice is a shot where the ball sets off to the left of the target line (still in terms of right-handed players) and swerves in the air to finish right off the target line. The ball has the same flight as the back-spin shot in table tennis. To play this shot the table tennis bat is held open to the target line and the swing line is from out-to-in and the bat cuts across the target line under the ball. The ball swerves from left to right.

● THE SWING PATH ●

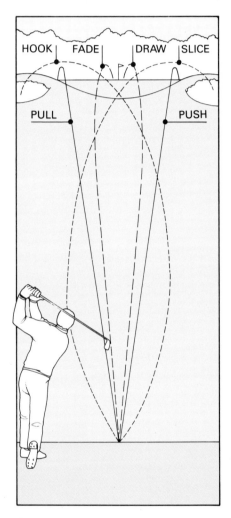

The golfing terms for the direction of shot.

● THE SLICE ●

1 This is the same as the back-spin shot in table-tennis. The feet are open, aiming left of the target line, with the bat also lying open.

2 The hands are in an open position at the top of the backswing.

3 To reach the top of the follow-through, the table-tennis bat cuts across the target line, putting back-spin on the ball.

● THE PULL ●

The pull shot goes straight to the left of your intended target line without any swerve. In table-tennis the bat takes an out-to-in swing, coming across the target line, but with the face of the bat square to the actual swing line. The ball would miss the table on the left.

● THE PUSH ●

The push shot sends the golf ball straight to the right of the target line. Its equivalent table tennis shot also flies straight and misses the table on the right. It is effected by an in-to-out swing path with the bat face square to the swing line.

● THE HOOK ●

The flight of a hooked ball starts to the right of the target line and swings in the air to finish left of the target line. In table tennis, its nearest equivalent is the smash, which has an in-to-out swing with the bat face closed to the target line, putting top spin on the ball.

1 The hook is closest to the table-tennis smash. The feet are closed to the target line (pointing to the right).

● THE HOOK ●

2 At the top of the backswing, the bat is on the inside of the target line.

3 To reach the top of the follow-through, the bat travels from the inside, at the top of the backswing, to the outside at the top of the follow-through. The table tennis bat turns over, closing the face as it strikes the ball, putting top-spin or over-spin on the ball. The flight of the ball is from right to left.

● COMMON FAULTS ●

You must analyze your own game to find any faults with your aim, grip, stance, the position of the ball or your swing to discover the cause of any of your own wayward shots. Listed below are some ideas to help diagnose the possible cause of the trouble.

You might *slice* shots because:

● In your aim the club blade is open to the target.

● Your grip is too weak.

● Your feet or body are lined up left of the target in the stance.

● In your swing, you open the club-face at the start of the backswing.

● Your wrists cup at the top of the backswing, which also causes an open face.

● You are starting the downswing with the right shoulder coming out towards the ball, causing an out-to-in swing.

TOP At the top of the backswing, the back of the left hand and wrist must be level. This ensures that the clubhead is square to the plane.

FAR LEFT If your grip is too weak, the club-face will open on impact, causing the ball to slice.

ABOVE AND LEFT If the wrists are cupped at the top of the backswing, the club-face will be open.

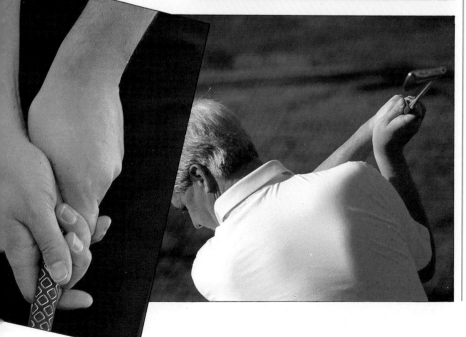

You might *pull* shots because:
- In your aim, the club-face is pointing left of the target.
- In your stance and position in relation to the ball, your body alignment is forcing you to the left and the ball is too far forward.
- In the swing you are not transferring your weight properly in the follow-through, but continuing to support your body weight on your right foot.

You might *push* shots because:
- In your aim, the club-face is pointing right of the target.
- In your stance and ball position, the body alignment is forcing you to the right, with the ball too far back from the centre line between your feet.
- In your swing, your body weight is being transferred too early onto your left leg.

You might *hook* shots because:
- In your aim, the blade of the club is closed to the target.
- Your grip is too strong.
- In the stance and ball position your feet and body are facing to the right of the target.
- In your swing you are closing the club-face at the start of the backswing.
- Your wrists are bowed at the top of the backswing, which closes the club-face

TOP If you pull your shots consistently to the left, it could be that your clubhead is pointing to the left of the target at the address position.

CENTRE LEFT Make sure that your wrists are not bowed at the top of the backswing, which will tend to make you hook.

CENTRE If you push your shots consistently to the right, your club-face may be pointing to the right of the target.

FAR LEFT Make sure that your grip is not too strong: this will also make you hook the ball.

LEFT If you close the club-face at the start of the swing, you will hook.

● AWKWARD LIES ●

You will be straying soon enough off the straight and narrow fairways of golf. Do not be too disheartened to find yourself with awkward lies. You may have graduated from pitch and putt courses on which the crisp shots and the soaring golf ball gave you an enhanced view of your ability. You may have come from the driving ranges where you found life and power in your hands, which must now be applied in a wholly different situation. Some of the world's top golf courses are designed in undulating countryside which the course architect wished to preserve, as a challenge to your skills and a pleasant sight to your eyes. He aimed to bring out the best in you. It is up to you now to bring out the best aim for him.

When in an awkward lie, do not be too bold, and watch where you position your weight. These cautions should come into your mind when you find your ball in two of the most awkward of lies: an uphill or a downhill lie.

● ADJUSTMENT FOR THE DOWNHILL LIE ●

1 The loft of a club is decreased from an eight to a seven or six, depending on the steepness of the slope.

2 The ball should be towards the back foot. Your weight is is in front of the ball. From this position it is easier to ensure that you strike the ball first and not hit the ground behind the ball.

3 Restrict body movement by taking only a short backswing, keeping the weight in front of the ball.

4 Don't try for too much length. Ensure that you keep your balance.

● DOWNHILL ●

You look at the target line with the ground flowing away from you in the downhill lie and you feel that on a flat fairway you might need an 8-iron, say, to pitch the ball onto the green. But you are striking down into the ball because of the slope. Depending on the degree of slope, that position is going to tighten up the loft of the club, giving it the action of a 7-iron or perhaps a 6-iron. It is the same as hooding the club-face over the ball, closing the face, and thus reducing the loft.

Assume a stance where the ball is well back towards the right foot so that you swing directly into it. Take care not to hit the ground first. If you hit the ball first and it goes up and away you will put slice spin on it, like the back spin chopshot in table tennis. The ball will go left and come back to the right. If the lie of the ball allows you to reach for a straighter-faced, less lofted, club, because the target is more than a long pitch away, aim further left. The slice spin should bring it round, if your swing matches your chosen club.

When taking aim, grip the club a little lower than normal – it's called going down the shaft. It will give you more control for this awkward shot. Keep your hands forward of the ball.

You must feel comfortable for this shot, confident that you will not lose your balance as you swing the clubhead through the ball. Flex your knees – the right one will be bent inwards a little to balance your weight on the slope. Begin with a short backswing. Take the club back with your arms, not your shoulders, on a line suggested by the slope of the ground. Keeping your head still will bring confidence that you will not lose your balance as you strike downwards and through the ball.

● ADJUSTMENT FOR THE UPHILL LIE ●

1 The angle of the clubhead is increased. A seven-iron will become an eight- or even a nine-iron, depending on the steepness of the slope.

2 The ball should be in front of the centre line, enabling you to swing through, with the slope, to achieve maximum lift.

The length of the backswing should be determined by the angle of the slope. You must not swing so far back as to lose your balance.

● UPHILL ●

The slope increases the loft of the club so that a 7-iron played on an upward slope will carry the ball the shorter distance of an 8-iron or, on a steeper slope, a 9-iron.

You are swinging into a ball on an uphill slope. This will have the effect of increasing the loft on the club-face. This makes you think twice about club selection. It is not enough to choose a club which will suit the distance. It has to carry enough loft to lift the ball clear of the slope.

Boldness is not your friend when you are facing a ball with your left leg and foot higher than the right. The ball must be struck on the up-swing. This will cause it to have a hook spin, so allow for this built-in movement in the flight by aiming off a little to the right.

Facing a steep slope, you will need height to clear it. You will be tempted towards a stronger club to achieve distance. Do not be too greedy: you may catch the slope and lose distance. Watch out, too, for that natural tendency to move your body weight into the slope on the downswing. This troublemaker means your downswing will lose its arc and will come in too steeply, 'de-lofting' the clubface to lower the trajectory of the ball, which will fly into the slope.

Here is how to play the shot. Stand behind the ball and picture the flight. Seek the target line. Remember the ball will move slightly to the left. Do not be tempted to be too bold. Take aim. Grip the club lower down than normal to give you a little more control. Take your stance with the ball positioned more towards the left foot than the right. Your posture will depend on the steepness of the slope, your left knee bending more than your right, so that your body angle is as near as possible to 90° to the slope. Keep your weight on your right leg so you may sweep through the ball when making the strike. Keep the backswing short to a maximum of a three-quarter swing. Swing through the ball, with a follow-through high enough to ensure that you do not lose your balance.

● ABOVE THE FEET – FLAT SWING ●

1 Take a more upright stance at an angle of 90° to the slope. From this position the swing plane will be flatter than normal.

2 The swing should be within your balance limits. The longer the swing, the greater the likelihood of loss of balance.

3 In the follow-through, keep your head still a little longer than usual.

● ABOVE THE FEET ●

Another tricky situation is playing the ball when it is above your feet, on a slope going upwards from left to right. Balance is always the keystone when building a stance for awkward lies.

Flex your knees so that you have your weight solidly over your feet and can feel that it is not going to slip onto your heels. Once again, go down the shaft a little with your grip to gain more control and allow you to stand closer to the ball. Assume a more than normally upright stance at an angle of 90° to the slope. Take the ball from a spot nearer to the left foot than the right, to help

a smooth action through it, when you strike.

The swing must be within your balance limits: the longer the swing, the more likely it is that you will sway away from the ball. The stance will give you a flatter swing plane and, coupled with the fact that the toe of the club will be slightly off the ground, the club-face will close slightly. This gives the ball draw – moving right to left in flight.

Your stance allows you to take a confident swing because there is no restriction on the body turn. With a maximum three-quarter back-swing, concentrate on sweeping the club through the ball to a good high finish.

● BELOW THE FEET – UPRIGHT SWING ●

1 To anchor your balance at the address, your weight should be on your heels. Stick your bottom out more than usual as you flex your knees. From this position the swing plane will be more upright than normal.

2 From this position, the hips will not be able to move, so concentrate on generating power from the shoulder turn.

3 As with shots from all awkward lies, the head should be kept still a little longer than usual to prevent loss of balance.

● BELOW THE FEET ●

When the ball is below the feet, that is on a slope rising from right to left, it presents the most awkward of the four lies discussed here. The amount of slope will determine the distance that you stand from the ball.

To anchor your balance, keep your weight back on your heels as you address the ball. Stick your bottom out a little more than usual as you flex your knees. You can feel immediately that this position will restrict the amount of shoulder and body turn in the swing and will encourage a steeper than normal swing plane.

Your balance is threatened in this shot. You have no shoulder turn to help your swing. You must leave that to your arms and hands. Spread your feet to provide the best chance of balancing confidently.

Aim down to the left of the target. This will help you to keep the clubhead square. Take your stance so that the ball lies in the middle of your feet, and grip the club at the top end of the grip, as you need to use as much of the shaft as you can.

Let your arms and hands control the swing without affecting your balance.

• BUNKER SHOTS •

Although the word bunker is said to be a Scottish term for receptacle, do not look upon it as being the trash can of your game. While average golfers curse their luck when the little white ball kicks off-line down the fairway and pops into a bunker, most tournament professionals shrug their shoulders. To them, the ball is in a position for an attacking shot.

Bunkers *can* be fearsome, like the infamous 'Hell Bunker' guarding the 14th green on St Andrews Old Course, or 'Hell's Half-acre' the biggest bunker in the world, at the 7th at Pine Valley, New Jersey; or they can be shallow traps laid well down the fairway to catch the wayward tiger-line drivers. Not only are they all shapes and sizes, but the sand within them sometimes differs even around the same course.

To discover what you have to beat, you need to be in the bunker getting the feel through your feet. But before you ever go into a sand bunker at all, there are two rules that you must always remember. The first is that you may only ground the club in striking the shot. If you touch the sand while in the address position or in the course of the backswing you will be penalized. When addressing the ball therefore, make sure that your clubhead is clear of the sand. It is better to hold it three inches (75 mm) above the ball at the address position than $\frac{1}{16}$ inch (1.5 mm) too low.

The second thing to remember is that when you have played your shot out of the bunker, always rake the sand flat, both where you have played the shot and where you have made foot marks walking in to play the shot. However, this carries no penalty, unless a golf club committee has made a local rule.

One other thing worth mentioning is that when you are taking your stance in a bunker to address the ball, you are allowed to twist your feet into the sand. This will give you a good solid base from which to start your swing, and it will give you an idea of the depth and texture of the sand in the bunker.

The club for bunker play is, not unnaturally, the sand wedge, which is designed with three outstanding features: it is the heaviest club, which helps when striking down and into the sand; it has the greatest loft of all golf clubs to help lift the sand and ball up and away; and it has a flange which will level off the clubhead as it travels under the ball.

TOP AND ABOVE Imagine there is a circle around the ball which is the white of a fried egg; the ball itself is the yolk. When taking the shot, strike the sand behind the ball, sending the sand and the ball onto the green.

• BUNKER SHOT STANCE •

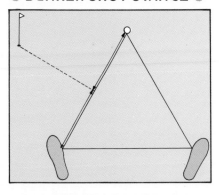

For the standard bunker shot, visualize a line from the flag bisecting the triangle of feet and ball.

LEFT When addressing the ball for a sand shot, make sure the club is well clear of the sand.

LEFT It is a penalty for the clubhead to touch the sand, except when it actually strikes at the ball.

LEFT You are allowed to twist your feet into the sand to give you a solid base from which to start your swing. It also gives you an idea of the depth and texture of the sand.

● THE SHORT BUNKER SHOT ●

1 Remember that a trap shot can be an attacking shot.

2 Even in a bunker, stand behind the ball and always look for the target line.

3 Always point to the left of the target with both feet and shoulders.

4 The wrist must break early in the swing.

5 The length of backswing will be determined by the length of the shot.

6 Strike the sand behind the ball.

7 Make sure you follow through to control the flight of the ball.

● THE SUNNY-SIDE UP SHOT ●

When you see your ball roll or pitch into a sand trap, do not let your hopes fade. For you could be facing a 'sunny-side up' shot. Look at the ball lying in the bunker and imagine it is a fried egg lying there sunny-side up. The ball is the yolk and the sand circle around it the white. Take your sand wedge and note the big flange on it. You have to use this to take that fried egg out of the sand, white and yolk together.

Line up your feet and your shoulders, pointing slightly left of the target – an out-to-in plane. When you come through the shot, as you must, the flanged clubhead will cut nicely under the fried egg, exploding it onto the green. The strength of the shot and the amount of sand you take will determine its length.

● THE SHORT BUNKER SHOT: FRONT VIEW ●

1 The ball is not too badly plugged and has not landed on a slope, two of the worst things that can happen in the bunker.

2 The swing is upright to ensure lift.

**STRIKING THE BALL
(RULE 14)**
If you are caught in the bunker, you cannot use your club like a spoon: remember that the ball must be 'fairly struck at'. (For the truly devious among you, note that rule 13–3 forbids the building of a neat sand platform for your feet, which could help when you play from a slope!)

3 Because you want to get maximum lift, you should hit slightly across the ball, rather than straight through it. The ball is forward and the line of the feet and shoulders aims off to the left.

4 Try to keep the swing at an even pace throughout, to avoid misdirecting the ball.

● THE EXPLOSION SHOT ●

To explode out of the sand, lay your clubhead open with the bottom of the blade square to the target. This will force your hands to be forward of the ball. Aim your feet left of the target and open to the target line, with your shoulders pointing in the same direction. Shuffle your feet into the sand. This will put them slightly below the ball and help you in taking some sand with the shot. This stance should allow the ball to be well forward. Take the hands down the club grip just a little. The swing should be long and slow, rather than a short, quick swing. Swing the club back smoothly, breaking the wrists almost straight away to the top of the backswing. Then bring the clubhead down and across the line striking the sand two inches (50 mm) behind the ball to send the sand and the ball onto the green. *The clubhead does not hit the ball.* It is the force of it striking down into the sand behind the ball which propels the ball upward onto the green.

TOP RIGHT When playing up the slope from a bunker you cannot use the sunny-side up shot without adjustment, because there is no cushion of sand behind the ball. Try to compensate for this by leaning with the slope as far as possible so that, in effect, you are playing from flat sand.

TOP FAR RIGHT You are permitted to settle your feet into the sand; this will give you a firmer base and some feel for the sand's consistency.

RIGHT When the ball is plugged, take up a square stance and hit through the sand with the clubhead square to the ball.

FAR RIGHT If you are in a fairway bunker and therefore want to gain distance with the shot, it is better to stand on the surface of the sand to avoid giving the ball excessive loft.

● THE LONG BUNKER SHOT ●

Bunkers are placed as hazards around the course, not only to guard the green, but to make approach shots more challenging. You will need to know how to play the long shot out of one of these bunkers, where the object is to get the greatest distance.

The club you need must be able to achieve the maximum distance but must also be able to lift the ball clear of the bunker wall. Long bunkers, sometimes laid to trap the long hitter, have low walls so you may be safe playing a mid iron or even a longer iron. Do not gamble by taking a club which has to be perfectly struck to be safe. Play the percentage game. Remember that with this shot, if you hit the sand before the ball, you will lose many yards. Think of a clean hit.

In taking up your stance do not shuffle the feet deep into the sand to make a deep base. This will set you too low and lessen your chance of clearing the lip of the bunker cleanly. Just twist the soles of your shoes into the sand to get a firm base from which to swing. Take a stance so that the ball is positioned towards the front foot, your knees bent only slightly to keep the swing above the ground. Look at the top of the ball rather than behind it. This will further help you to achieve a clean hit. Employ a full follow-through.

GAINING DISTANCE FROM THE BUNKER

1 The disciplines involved in this shot are no different from any other shot you play. Stand behind the ball looking towards the target. Find the target line.

2 Address the ball, making sure that the clubhead does not touch the sand.

3 and **4** Stand more upright than usual, looking at the top of the ball.

5 and **6** Don't over-swing, as this will cause a swaying movement.

7 For the long sand shot, a high follow-through will help ensure a good, clean hit and achieve maximum distance.

ABOVE The rough at La Manga golf club is not severe; courses in a dry climate do not have the long summer grass found off many European fairways.

OPPOSITE If you are unlucky enough to land in a divot, use a club with more loft and take up a stance with the ball well back toward the inside of the right shoe. This will help you to achieve a more effective chopping action, driving the clubhead down and through the ball.

● FROM THE ROUGH ●

When you find yourself in the rough, the only plan you should have in your mind is to get out. Be satisfied to find a line which will get you back on the fairway. Do not be too ambitious.

Your normal, smooth, free swing can spell danger. The clubhead arc will shave the ground at the start of the backswing, at the bottom of the downswing and at the beginning of the follow-through. If the rough is thick, it will tangle the clubhead causing problems with the shot. You must visualize an action which will strike into the back of the ball, without getting the clubhead caught up in the grass. You must strike down into the ball on a steeper arc than normal. Select a lofted club. This will help to get more flight.

If the rough is slight, take the ball in the middle of a slightly open stance. The thicker the rough gets, the further back from the ball your stance should be.

Grip the club down the shaft a little for more control, but do not attempt a full swing. A three-quarter swing will be sufficient — even a half swing might be best for the job. And don't worry about the follow-through — just let it happen. Indeed sometimes you might not be able to follow through at all because of the lie.

The important thing is to concentrate on bringing the clubhead into the ball at an angle. The angle will be determined by the lie and the thickness of the grass around the ball.

● ESCAPING FROM THE ROUGH ●

1 (INSET) Line up the shot, looking for the all-important target line.

2 When addressing the ball, make sure you do not press your club down behind the ball as this could improve the lie and thus incur penalty shots.

3 Stand with your weight slightly in front of the ball, enabling you to strike downward, which ensures that the ball is struck before the ground.

4 Take a backswing which will not unbalance you.

5 Strike through the ball, keeping your head still to ensure a solid contact.

● LOW SHOT – STRONGER CLUB ●

1 You will often be faced with hitting a low shot, either under the wind or under some trees.

2 Look towards the pin, find the target line.

3 Select a club to achieve the required distance without using your full swing. The harder you hit the ball the higher it will fly. A stronger club than necessary, with an easier swing, will result in a lower trajectory.

4 Do not unbend at the waist as you go through the ball and don't follow through too far.

●Low Shots ●

Many times in your rounds of golf you will want to play a low shot. Perhaps overhanging branches of a tree are impeding your path to the green.

Remember that the harder you hit the ball, the higher it will fly. With this in mind, when you have pictured the shot and worked out your club selection, take at least one club stronger, or better still two clubs stronger, than you need. The more club you have to spare, the easier your swing can be, while still achieving the required distance. You will therefore keep the ball lower.

You will need to keep your weight slightly in front of the ball throughout the shot. Gripping down the club will help to give you a shorter, more compact swing. The tendency when playing from this forward position is to close the club-face, so aim a little to the right of target. Position yourself further back from the ball in your stance than you normally would for the club selected. Then swing nice and slow, keeping the swing short and easy, not letting your weight move behind the ball.

● HIGH SHOTS ●

If you can play high shots confidently, you can make nonsense of the planned hazards of bunkers and the natural hazards of trees which suddenly get in your way. You soar over them.

The rough guide lines for this shot are naturally the opposite of those for the low shot. The harder you hit the ball, the higher it flies. You throttled back the fullness of your swing for the low shot, now you open it up again for the high shot. The swing is full and firm, and the club is one which is going to make the ball clear the hazard. Fix it into your mind that you are going to do just that: clear the hazard.

Stand behind the ball and line up where you intend to fly and land the ball. Forget eating up extra distance. You are seeking take-off, flight and happy landings in this short-haul shot. With the shot picture in your mind select the club with sufficient loft for the planned flight. Take aim. Position the ball nearer to your front foot than you normally would with that particular club. When making your swing, make sure that the full loft of the club is square to the ball and your body weight, although moving onto your left foot, stays behind the ball.

The common error in making this shot is over-enthusiasm. Too much strength is put into the swing in an attempt to smash the ball out and over trouble, causing the body to lunge forward. This sway de-lofts the club, cancels out the specially designed asset, the angle of its club-face, and causes loss of height, resulting in too early a touchdown.

● AVOIDING TROUBLE WITH THE HIGH SHOT ●

1 You will need to hit the ball high on occasion, to clear trees or overhanging branches.

2 When standing behind the ball and looking for the target line, think height! Select a club to clear the trees easily and don't gamble.

3 Address the ball in a forward stance, keeping your weight behind the ball.

4 Don't take too big a backswing; as with all shots, balance is the important factor.

5 When hitting through the ball, make sure your weight is behind the ball to guarantee a positive strike.

THE UNWRITTEN RULES

It is understandable that you will be engrossed in your own game when out on the course: it is in the nature of the sport. But this is no excuse for forgetting that others will be using the same facilities as you, and that you have a responsibility to extend the same courtesy to them as you yourself would expect to receive.

The enjoyment of golf depends on the conduct of players and the courtesies they extend to each other. One of the most voiced criticisms you will hear in the locker room concerns slow play. The time it takes to play a round seems to be increasing. Another criticism is aimed at golfers who do not replace divots or rake bunkers after use. At all times you must show consideration for other players.

● PRIORITY ON THE COURSE ●

In the interests of all, players should play without delay. On the other hand, no player should play until the players in front are out of range.

Players searching for a ball should signal the players behind them to come through, as soon as it becomes apparent that the ball will not easily be found. They should not search for five minutes before doing so. Having signalled others through, they should not continue to play until the players following them have passed and are out of range.

When a hole has been completed, players should immediately leave the putting green.

TOP Always smooth over the sand after playing out of a bunker; a rake is sometimes provided for the more 'popular' bunkers!

ABOVE If you are playing alone out on the course, remember that you must give way to matches of any kind coming through.

RIGHT Take care not to remove divots when taking practice swings, even in the rough. Do not take practice swings on the tee.

● BEHAVIOUR DURING PLAY ●

No one should move or talk, or stand close to or directly behind the ball or the hole, when a player is addressing the ball or making a stroke.

On the tee, the player who is first off should be allowed to play before his opponent or fellow competitor tees his ball.

In the absence of special rules, two-ball matches should have precedence over, and be entitled to pass, any three-ball or four-ball match. A single player has no standing and should give way to a match of any kind.

Any match playing a whole round is entitled to pass a match playing a shorter round.

If a match fails to keep its place on the course and loses more than one clear hole on the players in front, it should allow the match following to come through.

Before leaving a bunker, a player should carefully fill up and smooth over all the holes and footprints made by him.

Through the green, a player should ensure that any turf cut or displaced by him is replaced at once and pressed down, and that any damage to the putting green made by the ball is carefully repaired.

Damage to the putting green caused by golf shoe spikes should be repaired on the completion of the hole.

Players should ensure that, when putting down bags, or the flagstick, no damage is done to the putting green, and neither they nor their caddies damage the hole by standing close to it in handling the flagstick or in removing the ball from the hole. The flagstick should be properly replaced in the hole before the players leave the putting green.

In taking practice swings, players should avoid causing damage to the course, particularly the tees, by removing divots.

Local notices regulating the movement of golf carts should be strictly observed.

TOP Never stand in front of, or directly behind, the player taking the shot. It is not just the responsibility of the player to avoid accident, but of the onlookers as well.

CENTRE RIGHT At most golf clubs you will not often be so lucky as to have the course to yourself. Do not dawdle on the tee.

RIGHT The green is the most vulnerable part of the course. Leave all clubs, bags and trolleys off the edge of the putting surface.

GLOSSARY

A

● **ACE:** A hole in one (more commonly used in the US).

● **ADDRESS:** The position a player adopts to hit the ball.

● **ALBATROSS:** A *hole* achieved in three shots under *par* (more commonly used in the UK).

● **APPROACH:** A short shot played from the fairway to the green.

● **APRON:** The close-cut area on the *fairway* fringe of the green.

● **ARC:** A clubhead's path through the air during the *swing*.

B

● **BIRDIE:** A *hole* played in one shot under *par*.

● **BISQUE:** A beneficial handicap stroke which may be used at any time during the game. But it must be declared to be in use before the hole is played.

● **BLIND:** When the golfer's target – green or *fairway* – cannot be seen from the ball position, the shot is said to be blind.

● **BOGEY:** A *hole* played in one stroke over *par*. (At one time bogey meant the same as par for the hole, but this definition is not now used.)

● **BORROW:** The ground or path taken when putting on a green with a slope, in order to compensate for the slope.

● **BUNKER:** A planned hazard filled with sand.

● **BYE:** When a friendly match is won early, the remaining holes are the bye and can be played as an additional informal match.

C

● **CARRY:** The distance the ball travels through the air before touching a *fairway* target or green.

● **CASUAL WATER:** Excess temporary water which is not a planned hazard on a course.

● **CHIP:** A lofted approach shot to the green in which run-on of the ball is relied upon.

● **CUP:** Another name for the *hole* cut in the green.

D

● **DEAD:** Describing a putt, or shot to the green, which ends so near the hole it is a tap-in certainty. In friendly games, the next shot is usually conceded and is sometimes known as a *Gimmie*, a contraction of 'Give it to me'.

● **DIVOT:** The piece of turf sliced out of a *fairway* or other ground when making an iron shot. All divots must be replaced. Any ball rolling into a divot mark has to be played as it lies.

● **DOG LEG:** A *hole* in which the fairway between tee and green bends sharply. These holes are designed to challenge long drivers to take a target line over natural hazards like trees.

● **DORMIE:** A player is said to be dormie if he is as many holes in the lead during a match as there are holes left to play. It is a 'cannot lose' situation.

● **DOUBLE EAGLE:** The American term for a hole achieved in three shots under par. British golfers call this an *Albatross*, but the term is spreading across European and Scandinavian courses.

● **DUFF:** To ruin a shot, usually by hitting the ground before connecting with the ball.

E

● **EAGLE:** A *hole* completed in two strokes under *par*.

F

● **FACE:** That part of the clubhead designed and prepared to make impact with the ball.

● **FAIRWAY:** The cut portion of the golf course, running between the tee and the green.

● **FLAT SWING:** When the club is swung on a low plane around the body the swing is described as flat.

● **FLIGHT:** The path of the ball through the air.

● **FREEZE:** An attack of nerves experienced by some sufferers during putting.

G

● **GIMMIE:** A conceded putt when the ball lies *dead* alongside the hole.

H

● **HANDICAP:** A figure allotted to all golfers so that players of varying standards can play each other. The figure denotes the difference between a player's average score and the *par* for a course and is the number of strokes to be subtracted from the player's actual score for a round, to give his net score.

● **HEAD-UP:** The fault of lifting the head to follow the ball's *flight* as it is being struck, or looking up too soon after the strike. This impatience spoils balance and ruins shots.

● **HEEL:** The part of the clubhead nearest the shaft.

● **HOLE:** The individual section on a course from tee to green; the target on each green. It is cut 4¼ in (108 mm) in diameter and 4 in (102 mm) deep.

● **HOOK:** A stroke which, for right-handers, flies first to the right and then back to the left of the target line. The opposite is a *slice*.

L

● **LIE:** The lie of the ball is its position on the course after being hit. The lie of the clubhead is the angle formed by a line through the centre of the shaft and the ground, when the clubhead is placed flat in the address position.

● **LOFT:** The angle of slope on the club-face which governs the height and distance a golf ball may be struck.

● **LOST BALL:** Five minutes is the longest time allowed for a missing ball search before the ball is declared lost. A player may, in his own interests, declare a wayward ball lost earlier.

M

● **MARKER:** A disc used to mark the position of a ball being lifted from the putting green for cleaning.

N

● **NAP:** The condition, growth and direction of grass on the green. It should be studied before working out the line of a putt.

● **NET SCORE:** The score made by a player after deducting his handicap.

● **NINETEENTH:** The nineteenth is the name commonly given to the club bar. If a match, level on the 18th, has to continue to extra holes, the next is called the nineteenth, and so on.

P

● **PAR:** The number of shots allotted for any given hole, or for the course. It is based on the length of the hole, and on its being played expertly, with two strokes allotted for the green.

● **PIN-HIGH:** When, after being struck, the ball stops level in length to the hole or flagstick it is said to be pin-high.

● **PITCH:** A lofted shot in which flight is sought, rather than run-on.

● **PITCH AND RUN:** A shot where the run of the ball is of great importance after the ball has pitched.

● **PLAYING SAFE:** Taking no risks and sacrificing distance to find a safe lie or line for the next shot. This is also referred to as making percentage shots.

● **PRACTICE SWING:** Players are allowed to take practice swings anywhere on the course, provided there is clearly no intention of striking the ball.

Q

● **QUITTING:** A player not following through a planned stroke is said to quit. The usual result is that the ball is stubbed or half-hit, and the rhythm of the shot ruined.

R

● **RUB OF THE GREEN:** Used to describe accidental deflections of the ball from, or onto, the target line during play – either luckily or unluckily for the player.

● **RUN UP:** An approach shot to the green made with a club with little *loft*, so that the ball hardly leaves the ground.

S

● **SCRATCH:** An expert golfer, amateur or professional, who has no *handicap* stroke allowance.

● **SLICE:** A slice for a right-hander is a shot which starts left of the target line but sweeps back and ends to the right of it. It is the opposite of the *hook*.

● **SOLE:** The base of the clubhead which is placed flat on the ground, square with the target line, in the *address* position.

● **SWEET SPOT:** The strongest part of the clubhead, but not necessarily the centre.

● **SWING:** The smooth action with which the club sweeps in an arc to strike the ball.

T

● **THIN:** When the ball is struck with the bottom of the club it is said to be caught thin. Instead of achieving normal loft, the ball flies low and often too far.

● **TOE:** The tip of the clubhead furthest from the shaft.

● **TOPPING:** Striking only the top of the ball. It results in a loss of *flight* – the ball just scuffles along the ground.

● **TRAP:** A bunker (US).

W

● **WRIST COCK:** The natural breaking movement of the wrists in the backswing.

INDEX

Additional photography: David Muscroft, p. 16.
Additional illustration: Dee McLean, pp. 59–62 (main illustration).

The author would like to thank the staff and members of La Manga golf course for their co-operation and hospitality.